Hands of a Lady

Caroline May Doig

Front cover photo taken by Clive Preece
Back cover photo taken by Jenny Potter

authorHOUSE®

AuthorHouse™ UK
1663 Liberty Drive
Bloomington, IN 47403 USA
www.authorhouse.co.uk
Phone: 0800.197.4150

© 2018 Caroline May Doig. All rights reserved.

No part of this book may be reproduced, stored in a retrieval system, or transmitted by any means without the written permission of the author.

Published by AuthorHouse 02/01/2018

ISBN: 978-1-5462-8748-3 (sc)
ISBN: 978-1-5462-8764-3 (e)

Print information available on the last page.

Any people depicted in stock imagery provided by Thinkstock are models, and such images are being used for illustrative purposes only. Certain stock imagery © Thinkstock.

This book is printed on acid-free paper.

Because of the dynamic nature of the Internet, any web addresses or links contained in this book may have changed since publication and may no longer be valid. The views expressed in this work are solely those of the author and do not necessarily reflect the views of the publisher, and the publisher hereby disclaims any responsibility for them.

They are not long, the weeping and the laughter,
Love and desire and hate:
I think they have no portion in us after
We pass the gate.
They are not long the days of wine and roses:
Out of a misty dream
Our path emerges for a while, then closes
Within a dream.

—Ernest Dowson

Introduction

O wad some Power the gift tie gie us, to see oursels as others see us! —Robert Burns *To a louse*

I was brought up in a single-parent family during World War II, and I had a very happy childhood. It does not seem to have harmed me. It taught me to stand up for myself and pursue my own goals. I am proud to be Scottish.

I worked in the NHS during a time when it was evolving. Although some of the changes were for the good (e.g., junior doctors' working conditions), some were not—the loss of the community spirit and support within the doctors' mess. Neither do I think that surgeons in training get enough exposure to difficult problems. I would be unable to work in the service as it is now.

I made medical history by being the first woman in four hundred years on the governing body, the Council of the Royal College Surgeons of Edinburgh. I never set out with ambitions in medical politics, but I did set a precedent. I also became the first woman to chair one of the main committees of the General Medical Council. Although a woman, I was successful in what was then a man's world—hopefully without losing my femininity.

None of my achievements would have been possible but for the assistance and belief in me given by my teachers and mentors. Foremost in those who helped and supported me was my mother.

> *Life is full of many small incidents and a few (very few) great incidents.*
> —Roald Dahl

Contents

1 Beginnings and Roots 1
2 Early Childhood/Enilorac 8
3 Schooldays 16
4 University 27
5 Junior Doctor 44
6 Surgery 51
7 Job Hunting for Paediatric Surgical Posts 56
8 London and Great Ormond Street Hospital 59
9 Manchester and a Consultant Post 69
10 Medical Politics 98
11 Travel 109
12 Friendship 131
13 The Men in My Life 144
14 Mother 162
15 Third Life 173

1

Beginnings and Roots

The family, that dear octopus from whose tentacles we never quite escape.
—Dodie Smith *Dear Octopus*

Family, however tenuous the connections, makes you what you are and what you become, with a little help from circumstances.

I was born at 4.00 a.m. on 30 April 1938, in my parents' bed at home in Forfar—the small county town of Angus, Scotland. It lies at the foothills of the Grampian Mountains and in the middle of the Strathmore valley, which has rich farming land and is famous for growing fruit. Due to its proximity to Dundee, Forfar used to be known for jute manufacture.

The night before my birth, Mummy darned a tablecloth belonging to her mother-in-law. I still have it, with a mend that is older than me! I was a surprise because everyone had been sure I was to be a boy. Names were chosen: William James Keir Doig, or Keir for short. Mother rapidly named me Caroline, from a wall at Cullen House; more on that later.

My father, George, was the younger son of William Lowson Doig ,a draper and Jessie Ann Thom. His parents were born and brought up in Forfar. George had trained in London as a master draper, and at the time of my birth, he was in charge of the Linen shop next door to W. L. Doig & Son, drapers in East High Street. He was tall at six feet four, and he was good-looking with spectacles. George was born in 1909. His hobbies were golfing (a handicap of three) and woodworking. His elder brother, Alexander, was a medical student Mother knew as part of a coffee group in Dundee. They called him Palmolive because of his smooth skin. Daddy queried just how well Mother knew his brother. "Only for coffee and as part of a large group of friends," was the answer.

My mother was the eldest daughter and second child. Born in 1910, her parents were James Keir, a headmaster, and Nellie (Helen) Desson. Both were dux (the best pupil of their years) at Deskford Academy, at that time a renowned school. They both went to Aberdeen University. Her mother was fluent in French and was a German speaker. Her father was the eldest of thirteen and was born in Aberdeen; her mother was born in Cullen, a fishing village on the Moray Firth.

James Keir was a big man in every way—tall, handsome, and with a large personality. A headmaster by profession, during the long time I knew him, he was always going to a meeting. His wife had been a teacher in both Scotland and the north-east of England. Because of his job as dominie (headmaster) in country schools, they moved around Scotland, and so all four of their children were born in different places. My grandfather used to say his children were born near either prisons or mental hospitals. Mother was born in Kinnmundy, near Peterhead in the north of Scotland. Alan was the eldest, and he was preferred by his mother due perhaps to World War I and the absence of his father. Alan eventually worked for Marks and Spencer in East Anglia, and he married Penny. Elma, the second daughter, also suffered as a result of this preference for Alan. She became a teacher after university; none of the family were at her graduation. After World War II, she settled down with her husband, Ted Adams, in Dundee and had three children. Betty, the youngest child born to my grandparents, was born just after World War I. She could get away with anything, and did.

As a result of the four-year absence in France of his father, Alan was spoilt. When at St Andrews University, he flittered away time and money, and he did not graduate. As a child, he told tales on my mother, May, causing a degree of mental abuse, I believe. Once at a film, which he and his mother saw, she was made to sit on her own in the cinema and then to walk home behind them in the dark on a long country road.

Things like that affected her in the long term. She had a poor body image, lacked confidence, and was unwilling to meet new people. Yet when she did meet someone new, she was the best of company and was very popular. She enjoyed botany, winning a school prize, and had a talent for drawing. I still have two paintings she did as a schoolgirl. She wanted to go to art school, but in the twenties this was frowned on for a girl. When helping out at home was suggested, she applied for a nanny's post in the Shetland Islands. She did not get the position, but it resulted in her eventually going to teacher-training college; there was no money left after Alan's time at

St Andrews University. She did very little work but became an excellent teacher. She enjoyed her time at the college, especially as a part of a group of friends (including my future uncle) who met for coffee. After qualifying, although jobs were difficult to come by in the late 1920s, she secured an excellent teaching post in Dundee.

At that time, my grandfather was appointed to a headmaster's post in Forfar, and the family lived in Orchard Bank on the outskirts of the town. As the new headmaster, he was invited to attend the Old Boys Dance at Forfar Academy. He persuaded my mother to attend in his place. She agreed if he would pay for new gloves, which were worn at evening functions. She made her own gown. She and her mother went into the centre of Forfar to the drapers, W. L. Doig, and purchased the gloves. It was known that these were the wife and daughter of the new headmaster, and they were bowed out of the shop by a handsome young man, later to be my father. My grandmother remarked that he was a fine lad to be selling ladies' knickers! Mother said she would be home early from the dance but was not. She was walked home with the same lad, George Doig!

Mother and Father continued to be an item. Amongst other things, they both played golf (Mother had a sixteen handicap). They married in July 1937 and lived in a flat above the main shop and dressmakers' rooms. His parents also lived above the shop, but on two floors behind the rest of the building. After the wedding in Arbroath (by this time, my grandfather was headmaster in Arbroath, his last move), they spent their first night as a couple in the George Hotel in Edinburgh, featured later in my life. They then travelled to London and honeymooned in Jersey.

Enilorac

I was born nine months later. Was I conceived in the George Hotel? I like to think so. Certainly I was a honeymoon baby. I have no memories of my father, only photographs and things Mummy told me. My father died in South Africa in 1942 during World War II, when I was three and a half years old. Before Father died, Mummy was a housewife and was friendly with Vivian and David Callender (owner of a haulage company in Forfar). David played golf with Daddy. The family friendship continued after Daddy's death because their only daughter and I were at school together. There is a picture of the two mothers and little Vivian and me at about six months old—two blonde babies in the park. My friendship with Vivian continued during schooldays, and we have re-established the connection since my retirement.

I am told that I was a good baby, rarely crying. When I did, I was left alone to fall asleep naturally. I did not speak until I was nearly two years old. It was worrying enough that my hearing was tested; it proved to be normal. There was no need to talk because all my requirements were met. One of the first phrases I said was, "Me a hope no moo-cows," and I am still afraid of cattle.

Daddy made many pieces of furniture, including a desk, a revolving bookcase, and a tea trolley in his attic workshop. I still have them. I was his baby girl, and so he made me a doll's house bungalow and some furniture for it. Unfortunately, he was never able to finish furnishing it. He used a scale of one inch equalling one foot—not the usual scale then of one inch to sixteen inches. The house was one of the few things he made just for me, and so I kept it. Later, it led to the start of a new hobby.

When World War II broke out, he immediately joined the Highland Light Infantry (HLI) during a business outing in Perth. Although Mother knew nothing about this until it was a fait accompli, the Doigs blamed her for him joining up and subsequently dying. Because of a diagnosis of cancer, he would have died anyway.

After training in Scotland at Drem, and finally in Dunbar in East Lothian, he was sent out to East Africa, attached to the King's Own East African Rifles. Mother and I (an infant under three years) briefly stayed in Dunbar in a boarding house run by a delightful couple. The husband was a carpenter, and I still love the smell of wood.

I was very fair with dark blue eyes, and so the soldiers called me the blonde bombshell. The officers kept any fruit they managed to get for me. On one occasion in the town, Daddy marched past us (I was in the pram) and barked, "Eyes right." They all gave Mummy and me a salute! I was very inquisitive, and so early one morning, I covered myself all over with lipstick—and I mean all over. A scrubbing brush was used to clean me up. After Daddy left Dunbar, we returned to Forfar.

I inherited from him tolerance; even if I do not like someone, I can be polite. Mother had a much shorter fuse. Like both of them, I am unable to sit and do nothing—I must always have something to occupy my mind or hands. She had a very short married life, in essence only two years before he was abroad with the army. He started off in Kenya and then went south through what was then Tanganyika, Nyasaland (now Malawi), to South Africa. Before he left, between them they developed a code, and although he could not say where he was, Mother knew because of certain words that were used. He wanted to return to South Africa after the war, but fortune had other ideas. He developed teratoma of the testes (cancer). Initially it was misdiagnosed as a recurrent hernia. It was far advanced by the time of the correct diagnosis, with secondaries in his lungs. He died in November 1942, three days after his birthday. Despite it being wartime, they had hoped to fly him home, but he was too ill. It meant that the last time Mummy saw him was in Dunbar before embarkation. He was hospitalised initially in Johannesburg but is buried in Stellawood Cemetery in Durban, overlooking the sea.

Had he returned, there would have been more children, I would not have been an only child, we would have lived in South Africa, and I probably would not have been in medicine.

2

Early Childhood/Enilorac

First the infant mewling and pucking in the nurses arms.
—William Shakespeare *As you like it*

Mummy and I were now on our own, and for the rest of her life, it was us against the world. I gave her a reason for living. Her sense of humour and having to look after me kept her going in the many hard times ahead.

Apparently when she received the telegram telling her of Daddy's death, I said, "Nat a matter, Mummy, nat a matter," trying to reassure her that it did not matter. Because they had a joint bank account, it was frozen until the bank received the death certificate in triplicate—from South Africa by sea, and during the war! No help was forthcoming from the Doigs, and the Keir's money had been squandered by Alan, her brother. Because she needed money she decided to sell some of the furniture. Harry Johnson, a golf friend of Daddy's in a protected job, bought his work desk. Initially without telling her, he put money into a bank account for her. Although she never used it, the knowledge of it being there as backup helped a great deal. Later, his son was in my class at school, having been born a few days after me. After the bombing of Clydebank, a distant soldier relative who had lost everything was given Father's clothes, to the disgust of Granny Doig.

Mother returned to teaching, but like her father before her, she was sent to country schools throughout Angus. This would mean for long periods of the day, I would be alone, and so I was looked after by my maternal grandparents, whom I called Ma and Bimmie, in Arbroath. At that time, I was unable to say the letter *J*—saying bam instead of jam—and so I called my grandfather Bimmie. This stayed throughout his life, and he would not let anyone else call him by that name. They lived in a large house with a beautiful garden which backed onto a park. Bimmie worked in his garden when he was not being a schoolmaster, and he had educated Mummy in wildlife and gardening. There is even a photograph of four generations of Keirs: my great grandmother (Bimmie's mother) in a long black frock with me on her lap (less than six months old), flanked by Mother and her father. It was easier for Mother to travel to and from Arbroath.

I was first grandchild and so was spoiled by my maternal grandparents (but not by Mother). Elma (their third child) married Ted Adams (later to be headmaster of Law Academy in Dundee), and she had just produced Teddy in 1942 (eventually a dentist). The rest of her family was Christopher, who died young in a road accident, and Jenny, later a respected lawyer in Dundee who sadly died from breast cancer recently.

I used the garden as a playroom and the summer house as a stage. I put on performances for Ma and Mummy. They had to walk up and into a row between the trees to get to the deck chairs, and then they had to endure my entertainment! Although I was on my own, I had a vivid imagination and was never lonely. Mother's brother and his wife, Penny, tried to persuade Mummy to send me to boarding school to give her more freedom. She did not wish to be separated from me, and so this was a ridiculous idea (but rather typical of them both).

In Arbroath, my grandparents had a lovely black Labrador called Rajah. Bimmie had always had a gun dog. When Mother was growing up, there was a black spaniel called Sammie, which sometimes shared her bed although it was not allowed. One day before I was school age, I walked across the park behind the garden and visited a friend of the family called Kalinda. She gave me some Christmas baubles (calling them witch's balls), which I adored. She told me not to tell anyone. When Mummy came home from teaching, she asked me where I had got them, but I would not say. She became angry and said that she would smack me if I did not tell her. I replied, "Smack me, then." Much to her own mother's dismay, she did, but I still would not say. A few days later, Kalinda visited, and everything became clear. Mother had no choice but to chastise me. I was determined even then.

The youngest daughter, Betty, was at home, and we had great fun getting up to mischief. I remember my fingernails and toenails being painted bright scarlet. There was a detachment of Polish soldiers stationed nearby, and some of the officers would play cards with my grandfather.

One especially visited a lot, and Wladek and Betty fell in love and married. Soon after, he was detailed to Monte Cassino—and survived. But Betty contracted tuberculosis, and there was no drug treatment available then; she died at home in 1944. I remember visiting her bedroom, and Rajah would put his muzzle on her hand and then rapidly turn tail downstairs into the garden. I was sure he knew what was happening. As she was dying, she said, "I'm going, and it's lovely." This has stayed with me all my life and has coloured my feelings towards death.

During the war, we all had gas masks in case of an attack. Children's masks were like Mickey Mouse but smelt of rubber, and I would not wear mine. When an air raid was announced, we would cram into a small cupboard under the stairs in Arbroath. I do not remember there ever being an air raid in Forfar, but then, it was not by the sea or a harbour. Because of shortages, much was make do and mend. To Mother's chagrin, I liked to show off to everyone my jazzy socks, a different colour for each toe and the sole—a rainbow effect!

Once Mother got a post in Forfar teaching in the West school, where Bimmie had been headmaster before the war, we returned home to the East High Street flat, but in the holidays we would go back to Arbroath and stay with my grandparents. I enjoyed play in the empty rooms upstairs, and I was even given a room in which to play. It had been for Bimmie's mother, my great grandmother, before she died. I would dress up in old clothes kept in a big cupboard. Ma (my maternal grandmother) said I "hitled" (badgered) her and twist her round my little finger so that she would to do what I wanted! Bimmie was a town councillor and so was known by everyone—or so I thought. I felt proud walking down the road with him. Once he introduced me to a famous footballer, Stanley Matthews; it meant nothing to me. We would go to the harbour, where he would buy fresh fish from the newly arrived boats for our supper. I always sat next to him at table and was given various condiments and chutneys to try. I still have a liking for such things so that even now, in the autumn, I make my own chutneys, especially unusual ones. I also search out chutneys in delicatessens. My friends enjoy tasting the more unusual ones, whether bought or home-made.

Bimmie tried to teach me how to play card games, to the extent of showing me how to cheat at pontoon. I was not very good at cheating but still enjoyed card games, although Mother's later efforts to teach me bridge were unsuccessful. She tried to tell me it was a social asset!

Mother and I went to Arbroath by train (which was possible then), and I would make up stories about the trees along the way—brides if in blossom and bridegrooms if evergreens. On arrival, we would walk from the station. Once, I rushed ahead and burst into Ma, saying, "Say hello to Georgie." She raised her eyebrows after Mummy said, "He's been with us the whole journey." This was my imaginary friend, so maybe I was a bit lonely. However, I liked make-believe

In Forfar, a young boy who would end up in my class at school lived nearby with his parents. His father was a bank manager with a large house and garden. Lewis taught me cricket and football, and in return I would make him play doctor and patient (he was always the patient). Once he inadvertently hit me, but I explained the bruise as having walked into a door. That is, until his mother dragged him

Enilorac

up to our flat to apologise and Mummy found out. Years later, we reconnected when I retired to Edinburgh.

Uncle Sandy married a Yorkshire lass when he was working in Rotherham, called Mary. Now the brothers had Mary and May Doig, which sometimes caused confusion. They had three children, and it was great when they came to stay with Grannie Doig. My new playmates were Rachel (about six months older than me) and Bill (about six months younger than me). Janet, the youngest, was a whole five years younger. She is the only sibling to have married and have children. We had great fun in the garden under what we called the umbrella tree. I was disappointed when Bill refused to eat his mince -made of earth! We also made the summer house into a shop with old dressing up clothes. We reversed our names: Bill became Llib, Rachel was Lehcar, Janet was Tenaj, and I was Enilorac Giod, which I liked. Within the family that is sometimes how I am named—strange, but our own idea. We all enjoyed make-believe and got on well with each other; we still do. At Christmastime, my Doig cousins would stay with Granny and Grandpa Doig, and we would get up to mischief, although Bill complained that I was bossy! Father was by this time in Africa, and so we sent a photograph to him.

When I was on my own in Forfar, I would play in the draper's shop and the dressmaking rooms. My head barely reached above the counter. I would offer to stretch things with the long tongs used for stretching gloves. I knew all the female assistants, and one in particular, Isobel, would take me to Keillers, a bakery and cafe. I thought I was quite the lady and would request a special ice cream, adding, "But I don't suppose you got it!"

Before going to school, I had my tonsils out at our local hospital, Forfar Infirmary. I was in a two-bed room and can remember having visitors, perhaps Grannie Doig. I had no problems but was very disappointed when I returned home to no ice cream!

Grandpa Doig had a white moustache that tickled when I kissed him. On one occasion, he allowed me to help him paint a garden seat as long as I did not put the paint on back to front—and I believed him! In 1946 when he was dying, he asked to see me—"wee wheaker" was his name for me—even though it was the middle of the night. I remember a big bed in a small room. Granny Doig was much less approachable. She did not consider that Mummy was good enough for her boy. She was an excellent baker, and I can remember being aproned in her very small kitchen and being taught to bake scones. She died while visiting the folks in Lenzie in 1952.

There is a picture of me in the Doigs' garden with my first snow. I am obviously not amused. Even though years later in 1947, when there was exceedingly heavy snow, a boy some years ahead of me built a snow house which I could stand up in within a snowdrift. I still do not like it. I have never skied or wished to; many years later, one of my juniors wished to teach me cross-country skiing, but it never happened.

Despite being an only child, I inevitably got what every infectious disease was making the rounds. Shortly before starting school, I complained of severe tummy ache and was admitted to a children's side ward in Dundee Royal Infirmary with a possible appendicitis. I was very unhappy and sent home a few days later with no diagnosis having been made. That night I came out in a typical measles rash. I had infected the side ward and was seriously ill for some time. It is possible that the disease affected my eyesight (I am severely short-sighted), and certainly my permanent teeth were damaged. I do not remember much of the illness until I started to improve. At that time, I pictured the bed as a ship and the pattern on the carpet a sea with various islands. Apparently Grandpa Doig, who lived downstairs, was very worried about me. He routinely went for mid-morning coffee across the road from the shop to Keillers with a group of cronies. They all knew that I was seriously ill and did not recognise him, even when he brought me the first snowdrop. When I was well enough to get out of bed, I could barely stand, and I can remember Grannie Doig and "Soldier Bill", a Canadian distant relative staying with her, trying to help me.

My teddy got whatever I had so he ended up with a rash (red ink). Although my rash from measles vanished, his did not. My dolls used to have blood "confusions". My uncle Sandy, Daddy's elder brother, was a doctor. When I was five, he gave a stethoscope, proper ear pieces, and a cotton reel for the business end. Medicine featured early on in my life.

Because cousin Bill never married, we are the last remaining Doigs, and there are no more Keirs from this branch of the family (Alan had no children).

Although I loved all my grandparents, I adored Bimmie.

3

Schooldays

*The whining schoolboy with his satchel and
his shining morning face.*
—William Shakespeare *As you like it*

I went to South School aged five years in 1944. This was different from the one in which Mother taught. In Forfar at that time, there were four junior schools: East, West, North, and South. World War II was still in progress, and rationing was in place because there were many shortages, especially of exotic fruit. On Friday evening, Mummy and I would go shopping. On one occasion in the grocer's shop, orders for delivery were on the floor near the door. In one were bananas—a rare treat only available for blue ration book holders (children). Mother loudly made a comment that the order was going to a butcher whom she was sure had no children. She was surreptitiously given a few bananas to keep her quiet. She wondered what would have been bartered in return for the bananas. Steak, perhaps?

Enilorac

Shortly after starting school, I got impetigo and mumps at the same time. I must have looked a pretty picture, with gentian violet on my face and a poultice under my chin tied on over my head! A consequence of childhood illnesses was that I missed a lot of schooling at crucial times, so I had problems with language and spelling. Mummy tried to help, and eventually I caught up with the rest of the class. She tried not to laugh when I had problems with "ee" as in beef, and I tearfully said, "The dog had a good feed of mince" instead of beef.

When the war ended, I could not understand why other children's fathers came to meet them from school, but mine did not appear. Often I would arrive home before Mummy, and I would hang around the back of the shop or at Granny Doig's if she did not have visitors. I had girl friends, but they lived some way from my home.

Once I went to play with one after school, forgetting that Mother would be worried because she would not know where I was. When I did appear, she marched me up to her then classroom (in a church hall) to give me the strap—but it was locked and she had forgotten the key. It must have got through to me, young as I was, that she required to know where I was and that she did not mind me playing. A few weeks later, I dawdled on my way home and she was not at home. I let myself in and proceeded to go to the bathroom. I dropped my underpants and was preparing to smack myself when she appeared full of apologies. Some parents had delayed her. I had learnt my lesson.

Like other girls in my class, I went to ballet lessons. I was head and shoulders above the rest of the class, having grown rapidly. When Mummy saw me clumping along with an equally ungainly boy from my class, she decided that enough was enough, and I stopped the lessons—but not my love of ballet, which still endures. Piano lessons later were equally unsuccessful, but my love of classical music continues.

I never had long hair or plaits at school. I only had longer hair briefly in my late thirties. Short hair was and is much easier to manage.

By the time I was eight years old, Mother had changed schools and was now teaching at South School, where I was a pupil. As luck would have it, she taught my class. It was not easy for either of us because she was trying hard not to give me special attention. I had to try to remember that during school hours, she was not Mummy. We used to wear combinations—a vest-like garment with suspenders sewn on to keep our stockings up. Mine broke, and so at break time I said, "Please, Mrs Doig, my suspender has broken." Poor Mother. I later found that I was allergic to nickel when we wore proper suspender belts. Pure metal like gold and silver is okay, but if a clasp is not made of pure metal, I have a problem.

One of my school friends who lived near me, Lewis, went home to his mother and said he was sorry for me. He thought my Mother was being cruel to me when she was trying to treat me like everyone else. Once during a reading lesson, we had to memorise the text and look at the picture opposite. On closing the book, she would then quiz us. The story was about a sultan and his harem. "What was the sultan's wife called?" I was the only one to put up a hand, and so she had to ask me. I knew it was something to do with cooking, so with a gulp, I blurted out, "Currant."

Enilorac

She had great difficulty in not laughing—it was of course Sultana.

By 1947, the headaches that Mother had had since childhood became excruciating, and she was diagnosed as having mastoiditis, an abscess in the bone behind the ear that was liable to spread to the brain. Surgery was urgently required, but she put it off until the summer holidays. She was very seriously ill because the bone had worn very thin; that she could have developed meningitis and died. This was at a time when antibiotics were in their infancy. My memory of this time is her sitting up in bed in hospital with a turban round her head, and I thought she was never going to come home. Her nurse said that she never wanted to see a child's face like that again. I stayed with Ma and Bimmie in Arbroath, and they tried to cheer me up by taking me to the circus, Bertram Mills. It did not help. I would write sorrowful letters to her in hospital. On release from hospital, she was totally deaf in one ear, and her balance was very bad. One of the ministers who attended the school where she was then teaching pontificated, "The sins of the fathers …" suggesting that she had been drunk resulting in her unsteadiness. All he had to do was ask what the problem was: imbalance following the operation. Unfortunately, this put Mummy against most ministers and the church.

At school, I did quite well until the age of nine or ten, when I had problems reading the blackboard. As a bright child, I was near the back of the classroom. The teacher, brought back from retirement because of shortages during the war, intimated to Mother that I was not seeing properly. Mummy had had dealings with her many years before in Dundee and did not like her, and so she was inclined to disbelieve her. She marched me off to the optician and was horrified to discover that I was extremely short-sighted and urgently required spectacles. Poor Mother. I have remained short-sighted and am almost blind without my glasses.

During my time at university, our ophthalmology teacher offered us contact lenses, which had only started to be produced. Now for the first time, I could see when I swam. At first I had the large haptic type, but they made me goggle-eyed, so I soon got the micro ones. Later, I found that I could see better when wearing my lenses. While working in London, small holes had to be bored into them because I did not blink enough and was prone to infection in the eyes. Towards the end of my consultant post, I even had varifocal lenses. With different lenses in each eye, the brain has to adapt, and it did. Now that I have retired, I have become lazy and have reverted to wearing glasses, but for nearly forty years I was a happy contact lens wearer. I sometimes take off my spectacles to do intricate embroidery, much to the amusement of my friends.

I was growing fast to eventually be six feet tall—not surprising with a father who was six feet four and a mother at five feet ten. This meant I outgrew clothes and my strength. Clothes, especially shoes, were difficult to come by and were expensive. Mother suggested I go to Clydebank, famous then for ship building, to get my shoes. I was taller than all my classmates, both boys and girls. Only once in junior school did I win a race, and Mummy would not believe it—I always came in last.

Towards the end of junior school, I was visiting one of the girls in my class (she was Polish and was the one who introduced me to Turkish coffee) when I fell off a lawn in the dark. Near the house, the grass was at normal height, but at the bottom of the hill, there was a distinct difference between the lawn and the path. I hobbled home with difficulty, and the next day we discovered I had displaced the epiphisis (the growing part of the bone) of my left ankle. This limited me somewhat, and it remained a weak area.

I did well in what was then the eleven plus examination, and I moved in 1950 to senior school, Forfar Academy, concentrating on maths and science. During school holidays, we went to Arbroath. Both during the war and after, we occasionally travelled to Cullen on the Moray Firth. The picturesque fishing village (now sadly no more fishing) was where my maternal grandmother, Ma, had been born. As well as her relatives, Mother knew the wife of the factor for Cullen House. On a wall of Cullen House, there is a plaque detailing that the house had been built by James Stewart and his wife, Caroline. Mother had seen this when younger and liked the name—hence my name. Money was scarce, and so we lived with the relatives, with two of us sleeping on a three-quarters bed!

With the war over, I had learnt golf at Forfar Golf Course, where Daddy had played. We played golf in Cullen –myself badly but I enjoyed it. It was a challenging course between the railway and the beach, across gulleys and from high tees between huge rocks. Over the years, I continued to golf, returning to it on a more regular basis after retirement. I am still not very good but still enjoy it, as well as being out of doors.

I would swim near the Three Kings (massive rocks under which Viking kings were supposedly buried). At junior school and in Arbroath, I learnt to swim—one of the sports that I do enjoy. Mummy insisted I learn because as a young child, her brother had held her underwater! I would walk across the town of Arbroath from Ponderlaw Street (my grandparents' street) to the open-air pool. Even when it was cold I would swim in the open air pool. The professional at the pool had been an Olympic coach and wanted to train me up to a high standard to race. Mother said that it was my decision, but I had no wish to be competitive. I was never any good at team sports, perhaps because of growing so fast. The only time I was involved was one snowy Boxing Day, when the girls were short of a goal keeper—a dangerous position—for a hockey match against the boys' football team. Despite the ball getting bigger with the snow, I only let in six goals.

The first holiday after Mother's mastoid operation, we went to Newtonmore with Mother's parents. It rained all the time, and so we called the place Newton No More! We played a lot of card games. We walked, and Mother managed to play some golf.

I choose science subjects because by then, I knew I was hopeless at languages. I enjoyed history and geography but disappointed our history teacher by not continuing with her subject beyond third year, doing geography instead. Science was great, but English was a problem. To my chagrin, I was not allowed to continue Latin into fourth year. Presumably I was not good enough—my one disappointment at school—but I later resolved this. Our English teacher, Mr MacMillan, was keen for us to be involved in drama. One of the plays was about the introduction of the waltz. I played a spinster aunt (of uncertain age) to the main character. At the competition, I took the part of a Georgian lady (with

Enilorac

Mother's old dressing gown and a doily on my head). It was said, "But what a pity we could not hear her!" That was not a problem for me later!

Vivian Callender, whom I had known since we were babies together, had a pony which we were allowed to try to ride. Unfortunately, it flung me into a bed of nettles. I have only recently been able to stand near a horse without fear. We did not have television—very few people did then—but across the road from our flat, there was a furniture shop with these brand-new gadgets. We tended to have our evening meal on a card table at the window, and so Mummy would try to lip-read the people on the screen. The first proper television we saw was the Coronation of Queen Elizabeth. We had been invited by our friends the Callanders to watch it. Mother did not get a set until I went to university. My grandfather gave me a scarf, which I still possess, inscribed with "Elizabeth I, Queen of Scots"—which of course is technically correct. Scotland had never before had a Queen Elizabeth, and the monarch in Scotland is always the ruler of the people, not the land.

I was never a girl guide, although their hall was at the bottom of our garden. Instead, I was interested in the Junior Red Cross and wrote to the head office to find about a local branch, unbeknown to Mother. To Mother's surprise, the local organiser appeared at our front door, and I became a member. I thoroughly enjoyed this, and the training in first aid and nursing was very useful later. We took part in local competitions. I was eventually chosen to represent Angus at Princess Alexandra's first royal duty. She was patron of our association, and the reception was held in St James's Palace in London. As I was introduced to her, one of her ladies-in-waiting remarked, "What a tall girl." The princess herself was very tall. Unfortunately because we were in a group, I got to see very little of London on that occasion.

My first dance was at the school towards my final year, when we danced with the boys and male teachers. My self-confidence (never very great then) was given a blow when one of my classmates asked me to dance. As I stood up, he said, "I feel sick," and disappeared!

In the autumn we would go tattie howking (i.e., potato picking). On my first day, by the afternoon I was having problems finishing my patch, and so others helped me. The following morning, I was in agony. I received no sympathy from Mother because she considered me to be a poor specimen. When the pain persisted, she took me to the doctor and was horrified when he said that I had appendicitis and required urgent surgery. This was done in our local hospital in Forfar. My recollection is of not fitting on the trolley—too tall—and wanting to take home my removed appendix.

Most Saturday evenings, a group of us (mostly girls) would meet, go to the pictures to watch a film, and have an ice cream at the local Italian deli. On one occasion, we went to see "Auntie Mame" with Mummy and about six girl friends—and we all decided that Mummy was Auntie Mame!

At that time, we studied for highers. Our results came out on the day of a school trip to Rothesay down the River Clyde One of our classmates who had not gone on the trip was at the station, crowing about what he had achieved and letting us go home full of apprehension. A few of us did a further year (sixth form); in my case, I studied more science subjects.

Enilorac

During the holidays between school and university, a group of us—Evelyn, Helen, Isobel, and I—would play golf, cycling out to Forfar Course. On one particular day, it was raining so hard that golf was out of the question, and so we decamped to East High Street, our flat. What would we do? Someone suggested making Irish coffee, but we could not find any whisky. The next suggestion was gin and T, and so we made a pot of tea and mixed it with gin. It tasted like the smell of cheap eau de cologne! Mother arrived and, whilst laughing at us, told us that the T meant tonic. I have never been able to take gin since—a useful exercise.

Mother had acquired some of the back garden (due to Granny Doig having died), and so she was able to indulge her delight in growing things, which she had inherited from her father. Although I helped at that time, I was not very interested until much later.

Throughout this time and later, we would visit a distant relative, Lizzie, in Forfar. She had been born deaf and dumb and had gone to Donaldson's School for the Deaf in Edinburgh. She would lip-read and taught us sign language, which became useful later when Mother became profoundly deaf. We would take her to the films, which she enjoyed. It was necessary to write on her back with directions for the exit when we left the cinema in the dark.

Much of the time, I was on my own and would listen to the radio. Initially it was *Children's Hour* with *Toytown* and then *Dick Barton, Special Agent*. Now I listen to classic FM while driving. I was a keen reader, especially of series of books like Swallows and Amazons and the Chalet School books. I even made architectural drawings of a self-sufficient school. I would sit on the floor with the book on the chair, totally unaware of the world and people around me. During the time of finishing school and starting university, I did some nursing in our local Hospital where I had had my tonsils and appendix removed. The nursing was hard work being on a geriatric ward with heavy lifting. I discovered I was also allergic to carbolic acid after having to disinfect a bed. However it was good experience and made me appreciate the hard work nurses do. I made use of this training when I had to nurse Mother when she suffered from Sciatica – even giving her a bed bath.

During my senior school Ma (mother's mother) died of linitis plastica –cancer of the stomach involving the whole stomach. Bimmie (Mother's father) became estranged after that death but fortunately (for both of us), we were able to see him before he died of a kidney tumour in 1963.

I enjoyed my school days and made lasting friends.

4

University

Gaudeamus igitur. Medieval student song
Anonymous

In senior school, I decided I wanted to train as a doctor. I had wanted to be a doctor since Uncle Sandy had given me that toy stethoscope. I wrote to the General Medical Council to ask about requirements. By return of post, I had all the information I required, and so I told my mother, again doing things off my own back.

Now I could plan what subjects to take in my final years at school to be ready for university. The problem, as ever, was money—or rather, the lack of it. Mummy had given up sugar at the outbreak of war because Daddy had a very sweet tooth; so now she took tea and coffee without sugar or milk. She had disliked milk ever since she was given it as a child to counteract her vomiting, associated with the undiagnosed mastoid infection. Now she gave up smoking without any trouble and became very anti-smoking. She was still teaching and so had nothing to offer the powers that be who gave out the grants. I was unlike some tradesmen's children whose fathers could offer free goods, and so we got no grant from the Local Authority. Perhaps the Doigs could help? But by this time, they had no shop, so no help there.

My recourse was to sit the bursary competition run by the University of St Andrews. One of the questions in the physics paper was, "How do you prove that the moon is not made of green cheese?" I cannot remember what my answer was, but I was successful in winning a bursary for the first three years of our six-year course. The bursary was awarded by St Andrews University but was for Queen's College, Dundee, then a part of St Andrews University. Although it was not a great amount, it helped. I would have to pass all my examinations first time—no resits for me. I spent the sixth year at school doing further science to help with the first year at university. My highers results were good, so off to university I went in 1956.

At St Andrews University, students wore red distinctive gowns—the older, the better. Mine came from the nephew of a friend in Forfar who was now a surgeon in Glasgow. The way you wore the gown (on both shoulders, or off one shoulder) indicated which year you were in. They were very handy garments: a dressing gown, a coat, a groundsheet, and a bed cover. Although I had done most of the physics and chemistry, I knew very little botany (mostly from Mother) and no zoology. In botany, I sat next to a chap doing resits. Hector was to reappear in my life when I retired to Edinburgh. In zoology, I always maintained that the dead dogfish which we were to dissect bit me. It had a glass tube in its mouth, and mine broke, cutting my finger.

Enilorac

The first two years, I stayed at home, travelling each day to and from Dundee. This meant I had little contact with my fellow students and no idea of proper university life. I managed to get first-class certificates in chemistry (second place) and physics (third place) The class in Dundee was small, (some thirty to forty students), and even when we were joined by those who had been in St Andrews, we were only around seventy. This compared favourably with Edinburgh and Glasgow, where my cousin Bill was a medical student in a class of more than twice as many. The small number meant that we knew our fellow students well by the end of the six years. A third of the class were women—higher than the average percentage then. When I was on the University Admissions Committee years later in Manchester, well over half of each year was women.

In second year, we started physiology, pathology, and anatomy (which I enjoyed once I got used to the smell of formalin). We were lucky then to be able to dissect the body (mostly bequeathed to the department). Four of us shared the work, and so we really learnt the subject. Our professor was David Dow, an old-school teacher who could make the subject interesting with stories and descriptions. For example, our lecture theatre was the middle ear with "bloody pathology below" (in life, the major vessels). He described a coachman in Fife with Bell's palsy (a partial facial paralysis). With such descriptions, one did not forget relevant points. We would sing, "Yes, Dave loves us, his lab man tells us so" to the tune of the hymn "Jesus Loves Me". He would look at various muscle groups on hands and feet and remark on them. I believe he even did that when he first met his wife-to-be.

Caroline May Doig

In third year, I was tired of the constant travelling and hoped to gain more time for study. I stayed in West Park Hall, a university hostel for women, in time for the major exams of physiology and anatomy. It was much less tiring being in Dundee, and I had the opportunity of socialising and making friends with people from other disciplines. After dinner in hall, a group of us would talk and have coffee, and some would smoke -although I was never tempted to try. In lectures, I never sat in the front or the back. Being in the middle suited me but left me open to the removal of my earrings! I always wore interesting earrings, and the boys enjoyed pinching them, though I always got them back.

After the important second MB exams, the rest of the year joined us from St Andrews for, amongst other things, hospital training in clinical work. I became very friendly with a group of these "newcomers". Friendships developed with Jane and Edna (now sadly dead) and others. I had met Jane during the bursary competition papers. A Yorkshire lass, she is one of my oldest friends. Edna came from Dundee and lived at home. We were three girls together, and although we were friendly with some of the boys, it was purely platonic. Tom, from Blackburn, was small, and so he would sit on my knee—one would not have seen him otherwise. We would tango together, and it must have been a sight. On one occasion, he carried me out of the Students Union in a fireman's lift. With my bottom in the air, no one knew who I was. Mother organised my twenty-first birthday party at home in April 1959 with just a few close friends from my university class like Jane, Edna, and Peter. It was a great evening.

Second MB came and went with no problem for me, and now we were let loose on the wards. As we progressed through clinical years in various disciplines, I knew I was training for the right profession. But I was drawn to surgery, and there were very few women doing surgery at that time—in fact, there was no role model for me. Little did I realise that in time, I would become a role model. During summer vacations, we were sent to various outlying hospitals to hone our skills and try various types of medical careers. I can remember sitting at Forfar Station (then in operation), waiting for a train to Bridge of Earn to do a student's elective. I told Mother I wanted to do surgery and what it would entail: more years of specialist training and further examinations after finals (at least two). I told her that it would be difficult and that very few women were surgeons. She confirmed that she would support me and help if she could. We were encouraged then to do these student electives mostly in the United Kingdom. Now, most of the medical students do their electives overseas. One I did was in Doncaster Infirmary, where I learned all about catheters from a delightful Indian registrar. Although I was there during the time of the horse racing, I managed to miss the fun and games by visiting Felicity, one of the girls from my year who lived nearby with a house full of cats. Her father, a Church of England minister, took us to Lincoln and showed us the cathedral with its famous carving of the Lincoln Imp.

Somehow, Mother managed to get some money to buy me a car for me in fifth year—a black and white Triumph Herald called Sara. I passed my test the first time. This was very useful because by this time, we had to go from hospital to hospital for clinics in various subjects. I was very popular. I insisted that Mother should learn to drive, and she eventually passed her driving test on a snowy and icy Boxing Day. She could not do a three-point turn but told the examiner that due to road conditions, she would perform a four-point turn. On that day, one of my classmates, John from London, was to have lunch with us, and he was amazed at our hilarity. Now living near Stirling, where he had been a physician, he is another who has come back into my life since retirement. Initially it was with his wife, Maggie, but since her death, we still meet occasionally.

In final year, some of the sessions were on Saturday morning. On one occasion, I was due to have lunch with Mummy and so was dressed up in a smart black frock with a long back zip. At the clinic, which was about tuberculosis and X-rays, I was near the back because I was tall. Suddenly the teacher remarked, "Would the gentlemen at the back stop playing with the lady's accoutrements?" They had been trying to unzip me—too much of a temptation for them. They did like to tease me, but I suppose they knew I could take it.

We always took part in Rag Week, raising money for various charities. We dressed up in all sorts of costumes—gypsies or heavenly twins. It was always great fun because there was a crowd of us. When we were driving around Dundee to various clinics and departments, we had been allocated to various groups made up of people close to each other in the alphabet. The others in my group, mostly men, would rely on me to know where we went to next. One of those men was Humphrey, whom I also played golf with and whose daughter became one of my godchildren.

Enilorac

Throughout my time at university I was always near the top of the class in most subjects, especially surgery and pathology, which I also liked. In an oral for a distinction in pathology, I inadvertently called the examiner sterile instead of antiseptic. Professor Lendrum of Pathology looked over his glasses and remarked that he hoped I did not mean it! I graduated in June 1962 MBChB, having passed my finals the first time. I had never had to resit. Finals were not too bad apart from surgery, which by then was important to me. The external examiner, a professor from London, was deaf. Fortunately, Professor Donald Douglas was aware of the problem and helped out when he thought the external examiner did not hear my answers.

The day before the results came out, the year held a beach party at Carnoustie, a seaside town close to Dundee that was famous for its golf course. Despite the weather being less than warm for early June, I remember my friend Jane in a bikini walking along the beach with one of the chaps in a thick leather fur-trimmed jacket, gloves, and a cap! Between the results being announced and graduation, the whole year had a slap-up meal in a classy hotel, all dressed up. As a reward for passing, Mummy arranged for a local draper to have an outfit made for me. We choose the design and the materials. It was a cocktail dress with shoestring straps in a blue based brocade and a matching evening coat in blue satin. I felt like a million dollars and wore gold shoes. After the dinner, we had a party at the bungalow belonging to Felicity (she was the one from Lincoln). It was halfway up the Law Hill and well away from neighbours. The lighting was dim, and I was heard to say that I had never danced cheek to cheek with anyone before, which was true. Everyone knew whom I was with: a six foot six chap from the year above, Neil. The owner of the house reappeared later in my life when her daughter was a GP in Edinburgh, and Felicity would visit me.

The day before graduation, there was a garden party on the lawn outside the Students Union in Dundee. Mummy and I were all dressed up, and she was able to meet my friends from university—amongst them Tom. His father looked at Mother and me and said later to Tom, "You're a brave wee bugger." My quote in the year book was, "Up the airy mountain, down the rushy glen she dare not go a hunting for fear of little men." Well, he had given me a love bite on my neck at said pre-graduation party. I tried to hide it, but Mother said, "Couldn't he reach?"

I made many of my clothes myself, with Mummy's help; she had done the same for herself as a student. Otherwise garments would not fit me. Now I could have a dressing gown that fitted and was long enough, as well as summer frocks, an emerald green dress coat, and evening gowns. I even learnt to knit. This was surprising because when I was child, Mother had to turn the heel and finish my knitting for me at school. For graduation in St Andrews, we wore white shirt blouses which I felt I could not make. Of course I could not get one to fit in the usual shops, and so I ended up at a men's outfitters getting an outsized man's shirt (according to the collar size) to wear with my navy skirt.

The next day, the graduation was in St Andrews. For years, the only communication between the two parts of the university was by ferry or train. Once the Tay Road Bridge was built, the two parts of the university split, and Queen's College in Dundee became University of

Dundee. St Andrews remained but now has no medical degree. Students can obtain a medical sciences degree in anatomy and physiology and then chose where to get clinical experience, with most coming to Manchester through a special arrangement. The road bridge had yet to be built, and so we had to drive round via Perth. I wanted Uncle Sandy, also a graduate of St Andrews, and Mother as my guests. It was a good day.

Some years later whilst working in Great Ormond Street Hospital, I was awarded ChM with commendation for my thesis on wound infection from the University of Dundee at a ceremony in the Caird Hall in Dundee.

I had enjoyed my student days. I was now a doctor, but that was just the beginning.

Wall at Cullen House with my name

Doig Grandparents- William and Jessie Ann

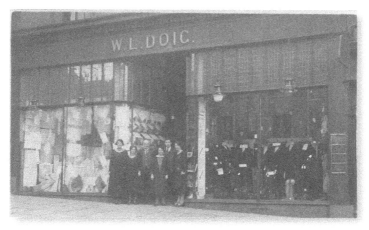

WL DOIG shop in East High Street, Forfar

Doig brothers – Alexander (Sandy) and George (on left)

Keir children -Betty at back, Elma, May and Alan

My parents to be

Vivian and mother on the right and Mother and me in park before WWII

Mother and me as a Baby

My father in Uniform- HLI

Keir grandparents – James and Nellie

4 generations - Great grand mother Keir, Grandfather (Bimmie), Mother and me aged 5 months

Teddy (Elma's son) and I eating our chocolate ration

Doig cousins - Rachel, Bill and me in Grannie Doig's garden

Photograph of me as infant sent to Africa

Bimmie and I (as a teenager) towering above him

Walking to open air swimming pool in Arbroath

5

Junior Doctor

Education makes us what we are. —Helvetius
De l'esprit

My first post in 1962 was as house surgeon on the professorial unit for Sir Donald Douglas in Dundee Royal Infirmary. It was excellent experience but was very busy, with only one Sunday in three off duty. After taking me to lunch one Sunday, Mother remarked on my tiredness. I said, "You should see the others!" At that time, we had no set hours and were paid a pittance, although we did get accommodations, laundry, and meals for nothing.

The firm, consisting of the consultants, senior registrar, registrar, senior house officers, and house men, were like a family. One knew if you had problems, there was always someone to call who would give you help. We wore white coats weighed down with stethoscope, tendon hammer, books, and notebooks. Once I was a consultant, I never wore a white coat because I felt it intimidated the children. There has been a change in medical training so that junior doctors no longer are required to do six months medicine and six months surgery, as we did, before acquiring full registration from the General Medical Council. Neither are they called the same: senior house officers, registrars, and senior registrars no longer exist—now it is foundation doctors. The doctors' mess no longer is available, with the subsequent loss of camaraderie and mutual support.

Sir Donald did general surgery as well as cardiac surgery with the patient on a bypass machine. I would be second or third assistant. A problem arose when I felt faint because of having had no breakfast and standing for long periods while doing very little. This tendency disappeared once I was doing the operating. Either I fell forward into the patient, backwards onto the bypass machine, to the left into the anaesthetist, or to the right into the surgeon! I decided to be excused. By the end of my time there, I could do minor surgery and even an appendectomy. For a lowly house surgeon, this was excellent experience. Now, such units have many more juniors, and the house man does not even get to theatre, never mind do any surgery.

All junior staff lived in, and we were well looked after by the housekeeping staff, even getting cups of tea in bed in some hospitals. This meant that the mess had a great atmosphere, and everyone was supportive of each other. Meals were in a separate dining room, and so patients could be discussed without fear of being overheard. This arrangement lasted into the beginning of my consultant years. Now everyone eats together in a canteen, and that exchange of ideas has been lost. There was no clock watching by any grade of staff; one would only leave the hospital only if all was quiet or satisfactory cover was available.

My first proper visit to London was with my friends from university, Jane and Edna, when we flew there—another first. I had been involved with a patient who was seriously ill with a very slow pulse most of the night. As dawn was breaking, I requested that I go to my room to change my clothes from slacks and a top over my nightgown. By morning, the patient was improving and more senior staff were available, so I could go on my mini break. I had not slept all night but did so on the plane.

Apart from the usual sightseeing, we went to the Cenotaph for Remembrance Sunday. It was harrowing but was something I wanted to do. We also watched the Lord Mayor's Show.

Junior medical post followed at Maryfield Hospital in Dundee, at that time another teaching hospital. The head of the unit was Dr Semple, but one of the junior consultants was Bill Stewart, who featured in my life. While I was working there, I was asked to look after one of the external examiners from Edinburgh during finals. He was very charming and asked me what I wanted to do with my life. Of course I said surgery, but that I knew I would have to fight for it. Back came the smooth answer. "I'm sure you won't have to fight for anything in your life, my dear!"

Mummy remarked that she had not seen me for some time, so I drove home to Forfar. Unfortunately, while going over a bridge, I hit some oil on the road and turned the car over. No windows were broken, and I was only badly bruised. My own hospital found the bruises when they gave me a tetanus injection. Only my pride was hurt. That was my only RTA (Road traffic accident) until after I retired. After a postgraduate lecture at the university, I fell down

Enilorac

some dimly lit stairs and damaged the same ankle that I had damaged as a schoolgirl. This led to a tear in the ligaments and a permanently unstable ankle.

After a year of living in hospital, I was ready to start thinking about the Primary examination prior to fellowship. This meant more pathology, anatomy, and physiology, and so I applied for a demonstrator's post in my old anatomy department. I stayed in Westpark Hall again, this time as a sub-warden. With very light duties, I had free accommodation of a bedroom and small sitting room. This was where I was when I heard about President Kennedy's assassination. I demonstrated anatomy with two other would-be surgeons from the year above. One, Derek, was a Jamaican and a friend of Tom's (my friend from my university year). He washed my hair on onccasion—I had been cheeky to him! By demonstrating anatomy to the medical students, we kept up to date with that subject and had only to relearn pathology and physiology. I sat and passed my primary fellowship examination in Glasgow in 1964. Now I was on my way.

Trying to get a senior house officer's post proved my worries about doing surgery. When I was interviewed, I was subjected to "You don't really want to do surgery, do you?" and "You're going to get married". My answer to that was, "Do I have to?"

Then I got a senior house officer post in Darlington (before there was a bypass round the town), working for Kenneth McKeown, a brilliant surgeon. Mr McKeown was meticulous about no blood being spilt—he would say that he fainted at the sight of blood. I learnt a lot but again had very little time off. One time, my hair was dirty, and the hospital dance was coming up. All day would be spent in theatre, and so one of the consultant anaesthetists washed my hair with dry shampoo before the boss arrived. The same anaesthetist suggested and let me sit on his knee (myself remaining sterile) when I flagged as second assistant during a very long operation. We were so busy that we often had beds in the middle of the ward and in the ward corridor. One GP did not believe me when I told him we had no beds, and he sent the patient in anyway. He did follow the patient into the hospital and was very apologetic when he realised I was telling the truth. I had no more trouble with him.

A lot of the doctors were Indian, and I learnt about curries, especially from a Doctor Doctor. The only unpleasant time was when I stayed with a married colleague whose husband was sitting an exam. She lived in a bungalow in hospital grounds and wished company. On return from operating, we had been burgled. Some of my jewellery was stolen, the worst being a special ring given to me by the husband of one of the girls who used to work in W. L. Doig's; it was irreplaceable. Some items were eventually found. Then the next night, on returning from a meal out, we found that we had been broken into again!

By now I realised that there was very little hope of me progressing in general surgery, and through Cousin Bill, in 1965 I got a post in the Royal Hospital for Sick Children, in Glasgow, Yorkhill. Paediatric surgery was a relatively young speciality, only becoming established after World War II. From the beginning, there had been women consultant surgeons in the speciality operating on children. I spent a year in Sick Kids hospital in the specialities of general surgery and paediatric orthopaedics. With Bill already a medical registrar in the hospital and cousin Rachel a senior nurse, we could have started our own Doig Institute—physician, surgeon, and nurse, with Mother for education and Uncle Sandy for administration. By now Uncle Sandy was Chief Inspector of Factories for Scotland. Two Doctor Doigs was confusing for some in the hospital. One paediatrician sorted it out in his own mind: Doig means dog, so we know what we call the female of the species—bitch. Not at all a pleasant comparison.

I soon realised that paediatric surgery was for me. I loved looking after children, and they did not pretend—they were either well or not. At that time, all the junior doctors lived in house, and so we had a great time getting up to mischief. At weekends we would have carry-out meals of all sorts. Unfortunately, sometimes the high jinks got out of hand. I was thrown into a bath of cold water. The tidal wave meant that the two "gentlemen" got just as wet as I did. I also made lasting friendships, such as with Ann McAra (later Ford), who later worked as an anaesthetist in Great Ormond Street Hospital. She is still my close friend.

Being in Glasgow was great because Uncle Sandy (very much a father figure for me) and Auntie Mary lived in Lenzie on the outskirts. It became a home away from home and cemented my relationship with my paternal cousins. I think he was proud of me—perhaps to the detriment of his own children. Bill became an excellent paediatric cardiologist in Glasgow, and Rachel was an excellent orthopaedic sister, only giving it up because of back problems. One morning when I was assisting the orthopaedic surgeon, I felt faint again and asked for a seat. I remember hearing Mr Blockey calling for a "seat for Miss Doig". Then I was flat out on the floor of the theatre, and someone was saying, "She's rather large to lift!" My colleague could not believe it when she was called to become his assistant.

Around this time, the hospital was found to be falling down (bad architectural planning), and so some of the departments were sent to various other hospitals. Initially I was sent to Drumchapel Hospital, a convalescent hospital where I was royally treated—given tea in the morning and mid-afternoon. Later, I was detailed to Stobhill, a general hospital. There, I mixed with non-paediatric trainees and had an active social life. Whilst at Stobhill, I assisted the senior paediatric surgeon, Wallace Dennison, who during the operation asked me what my career aims were. I told him paediatric surgery. He retorted that to be taken seriously, I would require both the English Fellowship and the Edinburgh Fellowship, plus an academic thesis on some research. Many years later, he admitted that although those details were true, he had been trying to dissuade me. He later supported me because I did do all that he had stated.

Eventually, the whole hospital occupied Ruckhill (an ex fever hospital), where we were until the new Hospital for Sick Children was built on the original site. Ruckhill was a series of old buildings, and so we had to go outside when moving between departments. It reminded me of tenements in Edinburgh and the old call of "Garde lou". I ended up breaking my ankle while running between the buildings in the rain—much to the amusement of the children because the doctor had a "stookie" (plaster) too!

Now I needed research and more general surgical experience so I could complete my fellowship examination.

6

Surgery

The surgeon must have the heart of a lion, the eyes of a hawk and the hands of a woman.
—John Halle *Attributes of an Ideal Surgeon*

After finishing in Glasgow in 1966, I obtained a research fellowship back in Dundee with my old boss, Sir Donald Douglas. The research was into wound infection, so I had some bacteriology to do. The thesis was for a mastership in surgery -ChM- or should that be mistress-ship?—on wound infection with reference to Staphlycoccus aureus. I was doing my research into wound infection on the wards and in theatres. I developed a sterile tent for testing various theatre garb to try and to prevent skin flake dispersal. This also involved me plating up and indentifying bacteria from swabs, and so I worked in a bacteriology laboratory—according to Mummy" my buggery". The Petri dishes had to be inspected every day. Other aspects were that I had to take notes of theatre activity (people coming and going in the theatre) and swabs in theatre and from patients. With all this and collating my results, I had very little time off—but very few night calls. The rest of the time, I acted as a locum registrar for people on holiday, keeping my operative skills up to scratch. This meant, amongst other things, doing the occasional operation list in Forfar Infirmary, assisted by a GP. Once we had a bleed during a varicose vein operation, which I managed to address with no help from him.

When the research was almost finished, Sir Donald arranged for me to present my results at a meeting of the Surgical Research Society in London. He introduced me to Professor Andrew Wilkinson of the paediatric surgical department in Great Ormond Street Hospital, indicating my interest in paediatric surgery.

At the same meeting, Professor Andrew Kay of Glasgow requested some of my slides for a talk he was to give in the States. He called me the "bloomer lady" because of some of the theatre wear we were testing. What an accolade for a research fellow! I also got papers published in medical journals.

Three years after getting my Primary examination in Glasgow, I sat and passed my Edinburgh fellowship in 1967. This was not without incident.

On one part of the examination, I was due to be examined by one of my consultants in Dundee. So as not to have undue influence, he arranged for me to be examined by a different pair of examiners. After lunch, I was allocated to a different table. One of the examiners (now dead) who had obviously had a drink or two at lunch kept patting my upper thigh as he asked me questions. Naturally, I froze and made a mess of my answers in the oral exam—my reaction being noticed my consultant from Dundee without initial knowledge of the reason. Fortunately, it was all sorted out in the end. Although I did not realise it, I was now one of seventy-six female fellows of that college.

One of the other consultants on the unit was Willie Walker, originally from Forfar. Despite trying to dissuade me from doing surgery, he supported me and later was instrumental in getting me on the Council of Edinburgh College. I do not think his unsuccessful attempts to deter me were because of my ability or lack of it, but simply because I was a woman. He wanted to dance at my wedding, but that never happened!

During this time, I lived in a shared bungalow with girls I had known at university (not all medics), and later I had a bedsit on my own in North Dundee. Mother was horrified at my untidiness and said that I was sordid. It was a very small room, and I was a big girl.

After two years, it was time to get a registrar's post in general surgery and write up my thesis. I did get downhearted when my applications for such posts were returned practically unopened. I wondered whether I should put C and hope that they would think I was Charles until I walked in the room. Eventually, I got requests for interviews from Aberdeen and Durham. The Durham one was first. The committee took a long time to come to the decision to offer me the post. I later learnt that the problem was I was female, and they had never had a female surgical registrar before. Interestingly, the next two registrars in post after I left were women! Much later, I was told that the Aberdeen job would have been mine. I did not know, and I would have not had as much experience of practical surgery because it would have been on a professorial department, with many junior doctors vying for operative experience. In Dryburn Hospital in Durham in 1968, there were only two surgical registrars (no senior registrar), and so I had lots of cutting and excellent training. We were on duty every other night, and that by the end of the two years, I could turn my hand to most general surgical operations. It was necessary to change into my theatre garb in the nurse's changing room because there was no separate changing room for female doctors. This did not change until well into my consultant post in Manchester.

I was lucky enough to have a room with a view of Durham Cathedral and Castle—a view almost as good as that of Edinburgh Castle. The people were friendly, accepting you as you were. We were a very close mess and had great fun and parties. One of the medical registrars was given a brace of pheasants by a patient, and so a group of the females cooked them in the hospital kitchen (with permission) as coq au vin and made a slap-up meal. The men provided the drinks and organised the venue in the doctors' mess This was before the time of the catering officer, who provided cold sandwiches for Sunday evening meal in the middle of winter. She even asked me what she could provide when we complained!

By now I needed a new car, and for the first and only time in my life, I had a sports car: a white Bond Equipe made of fibreglass. It was great to drive, and so I could drive up to Scotland and home occasionally. Dryburn Hospital (now a university hospital) had a regular succession of students from Newcastle Medical School, and so we got a chance to teach as well as learn from our patients. We also drove up to Newcastle to a regular teaching session for those of us doing

Enilorac

surgical fellowships, and we met the registrars in Newcastle to exchange ideas. My co-registrar was from South Africa, and he and his wife frequently entertained me.

During this time, I eventually got the fellowship of the Royal College of Surgeons in Lincoln Inn Fields, in London, having failed a couple of times. On one such occasion, I ended up having a drink to drown our sorrows with a fellow failed candidate from Ireland. Ray and I met again in Manchester. He and his wife became good friends. On the occasion when I did pass, in the operative surgery oral, I was asked to describe an open cholecystectomy, one of my favourite operations. I surprised the examiner by describing the operation, but with only one assistant. "How do you manage?" he asked. Some of us did not have the luxury of two assistants. I also managed to write up my thesis, and in 1970 I got a ChM (with commendation) from St Andrews University, but I was given it in Dundee.

Despite all this, I still had time to visit the many lovely places in the North East of England. One summer, Mummy (recovering from an operation) spent the summer holidays in Durham so that we could explore together. One holiday we sailed from Newcastle for Oslo. That was not without incident, as you will see later.

During this time, I gained invaluable experience for most of the problems in surgery, giving me an excellent basis for the more intricate surgery in children and babies.

7

Job Hunting for Paediatric Surgical Posts

Cornelia's jewels.
—James Baldwin *Short stories*

Cornelia's jewels were her children, whom she protected during a turbulent time in Roman history. Cornelia is, of course, an anagram for Caroline. I used this for the title of a talk in the Royal College of Surgeons of Edinburgh.

Now I was ready to think about paediatric surgery. My two years in Durham were finished, and I was out of a job despite having two fellowships and a master in surgery. Mother lay awake at night worried about my lack of a job, but Dundee and Mr W. Walker (one of my former bosses on the professorial Surgical unit) came to my rescue. I got a locum post in neonatal medicine for a few months—something that would be useful in the future. I also did some locum general surgery because it would not have been safe for me to be on call for neonates at that time due to my lack of experience with medical problems in newborns.

Earlier, Willie Walker had arranged for me to meet Professor Andrew Wilkinson again, this time in the Edinburgh College for an in-depth discussion as to what to do. He informed me that I should get a senior registrar post in general surgery before venturing into paediatric surgery. I had even suggested I could do pathology if there was no hope, but he told me to persevere. Now I wrote to him, having been unsuccessful when applying for senior registrar surgical posts—again because I was a woman. I informed him that I now had after my name FRCS Ed, FRCS Eng and was about to be awarded a ChM. He wrote back saying he did not approve of double fellowships, but he signed himself A. W. Wilkinson, ChM, FRCSE, FRCS. ChM stands for Master of Surgery (*chirurgery* being the old word), and FRCSE and FRCS were Fellow of the Royal College of Surgeons of Edinburgh and England, respectively. I kept the letter and much later teased him about it, and he laughed.

With no hope, I applied for a senior registrar post in paediatric surgery at Great Ormond Street Hospital (GOS), my only experience in the subject being my year as a SHO in Glasgow. However, because of my contact with the Professor, I got an interview in early 1970. London was experiencing a snowstorm, and so some of the people I was supposed to meet beforehand were unable to see me. Initially we candidates each had a long, intensive interview from the surgeons in the hospital—but then we were all told to go home. Back I went to Scotland on the night train. The administration should have kept us back to tell us who was for a second interview. Two days later, I was asked to attend again. This time, I saw no other candidates as I moved around the hospital. Only two of us eventually had another interview: myself and a very experienced male registrar in paediatric surgery.

I thought it was nice of Andrew Wilkinson to have got me this far, but I knew I did not stand a chance and so decided to enjoy myself. On entering the interview room, it was the full medical staff committee, with Professor Bonham Carter in the chair. No one had any questions for me; they had all been asked in the previous interview, or when we had met. Bonham Carter remarked on this, and I replied, "Was that a good thing?" I was out of the room again in no time, much to the surprise of the other candidate. After he came out equally quickly, we waited for the administrator. I was almost heading for the door when they offered me the post. For once in my life, I was speechless. Of course I accepted, and I was due to start on April Fool's Day, 1970. The female registrar who had followed me in Durham remarked that the other person was much better qualified and should have got the job! True, but it was better left unsaid. He did get a senior registrar post in the north of England soon after and was a consultant before me.

I returned to Scotland on the night train after a celebratory dinner with Ann Ford and her husband, Colin. Ann Ford (nee McAra) had worked with me in Glasgow Sick Kids Hospital. The next evening I went to a postgraduate meeting in Dundee and surprised everyone with the news of my success. Sitting next to me was my ex boyfriend, who was ready to commiserate with me!

8

London and Great Ormond Street Hospital

Hell is a city much like London, a populous and smoky city.
   —Alfred, Lord Tennyson *Peter Bell the third*

In London at the beginning of April 1970, I started by living in a flat near the hospital in Judd Street, provided by the hospital. I drove from Forfar with my car full, with only enough space for me in the driver's seat. Whilst in Durham, I had subscribed to a monthly Cordon Bleu cooking magazine. Apart from the recipes, there were special offers of kitchen paraphernalia—pots, pans, china, and cutlery at very reasonable prices. Some time before, a local electricity salesman had allowed us to buy some white goods before the prices went up (refrigerator, freezer, and washing machine), and so I had collected quite a lot, which were lodged in my bedroom at home in Forfar. I had Mother's help with things I did not have, and of course linen (bed and otherwise) from what had been Father's shop. I had enough to make the flat a home. The first night after I arrived, James Dickson (a junior consultant) and his wife, Jean, very kindly gave me a welcoming meal.

Working in GOS meant that there was very little time for leisure, although occasionally we organised parties. When I first started to work in GOS, I was in a flat in the King's Cross area that was about ten minutes' walk to the hospital and not one of the best areas in London. Once when running to an emergency at the hospital from my flat, a man stopped me and asked if I would like him to drop his trousers. When a flat in the hospital environs became available, I pointed out to the administrators that I urgently required to be within the hospital. He replied, saying that the flat which was free had been ear-marked for a medical registrar who was married with family. I countered that I was on call for a week every three weeks, and she was on call only every six weeks, adding, "So I have to get pregnant, then." I made no mention of marriage. Flustered, he gave in, and I got the flat.

My first morning as a senior registrar on the staff of the hospital I was met by a staff nurse offering me a cup of coffee. Life was going to be okay. We would get all sorts of unusual cases as a specialist hospital, and so when I admitted a patient with appendicitis—a rarity in GOS—the nurses vied with each other to see the operation. Excellent nurses and superb sisters meant that support was always available. Over my five years (four of them in London), I rotated round all the general paediatric surgeons: Harold Nixon (gastrointestinal problems), Herbert Eckstein (spina bifida patients), David Innes Williams (urology), and finally

Andrew Wilkinson himself (nutrition and gastrointestinal). All were excellent surgeons with individual traits and skills. Harold Nixon was from Newcastle, and my saving grace was the fact that although I was Scottish, I had worked in Durham. David Innes Williams had an international reputation, and we often had lots of overseas visitors crowding in on us at the operating table. I would use my elbows quite a lot, not caring where they landed. During my time with him, I made friends with an Indian doctor destined to be a urologist in Bombay (Mumbai), and he is still in contact with me.

Problems beyond our control were strikes and fuel shortages leading to electricity cuts—a problem for newborns in incubators. We were on call for a week at a time, and the senior registrar on call, the surgical admitting officer (SAO), went round the hospital identifying empty or potential empty beds for admissions not necessarily on the admitting ward. The top floor of the hospital was given over to private beds, which were often full. When I requested a bed on the private ward, I was rudely told no way, until I pointed out that it was for a royal patient. Then suddenly a bed (in fact, a whole side ward) became available.

I started with David Waterson (son of a professor in St Andrews university), who was a general paediatric surgeon and a cardiac surgeon. He had two different teams: myself on the general side, and on the cardiac side a variety of overseas fellows. One such was Keith Ashcraft, whom I met again on my later visit to the United States of America. He used to say that we held hands inside the patient when operating for a hiatus hernia. Ian Breckenridge, who had been my registrar when I was a houseman in Dundee, was in the department for a time. When in Dundee, he was required to slap a hysterical patient, but he inadvertently sent my spectacles flying with the end of his swing. Another was Yarda Stark from Czechoslovakia, who went to the States for further training and the possibility of a senior post. On his return for an interview for a consultant post in GOS, he said, "The bloody foreigner won't get it," but of course he did. We remained good friends even after the death of his wife, Olga. I have met him again since retiring, the last time at a lunch just before he married Shelagh, his new wife.

Working with Harold Nixon gave me excellent experience in bowel problems, and Herbert Eckstein did surgery on Spina Bifida patients. The time with D. I. Williams was superb because he was an excellent urologist and good teacher. During my time, I produced a variety of papers with others on various subjects. One paper, on laryngeal stenosis, was alluded to when a new technique was developed many years later.

Working with Andrew Wilkinson was excellent, and I also gained experience in treating burns. He did not suffer fools gladly, and one had to stand one's ground. On one occasion, Sister and I did not want him to operate on a particular child. We thought we were winning by subtle suggestion—until he turned to us and said, "I'm still going to operate." He knew what we were thinking!

Children bounce back after surgery to the point that they may be standing at the end of the cot in the afternoon after major surgery in the morning, to the amazement of visiting adult surgeons who would not believe me. Once a year, the professorial department had a Chinese meal in Soho, including the research as well as clinical personnel, to help the department bond. I developed a liking for Chinese food, which came in useful later when I travelled to the Far East.

I got the experience of the usual congenital abnormalities found in newborns, but I also saw some of the rarer ones. Despite not being a cardiothoracic trainee, I was involved with a patient with the heart lying outside the body. David Waterson calmly sorted it out with help from the cardiac senior registrar and me—a once-in-a-lifetime experience. There were three senior registrars. One of my colleagues was Leela Kapila, from India and an excellent surgeon. We remained friends even after she got the post in Nottingham for which I had applied. Later, she became a council member and then vice president of the English College of Surgeons in London. I meet her and her husband, Bob, at seniors' meetings at that college.

On one occasion, an infant of African origin was sent to St Thomas' Hospital for a lymphogram. This necessitated an intravenous injection of methylene blue. On return from St Thomas', because of his dark skin and the dye, he looked cyanosed and extremely ill. The junior doctor immediately sent out a cardiac arrest call, necessitating the presence of both senior registrars, surgical and medical. The latter said, "This child has not died—he is dyed!"

My mother had retired, and she would spend the winter months with me in my flat, looking after me and others, including Ann's new baby. Ann was a close friend with whom I worked in Glasgow before she followed me to GOS as an anaesthetic trainee. Mother and I would return to Scotland in late spring, seeing much of England as we zigzagged our way north homewards to Scotland. We also spent time in the Cotswolds and the West Country. Getting out of London was the only way to not be called out. Although we were on call most of the time, it was supposedly a week every three weeks

The hospital had a dinner every year in the autumn in one of the livery halls in the city. The consultants and junior staff attended, making it was a grand affair: all dressed up and hair intricately done. My hairdresser at the time was keen to experiment, and I let him. He went to the extent of emphasising a streak of grey hair that I had developed in my late twenties. The hairdresser enjoyed making hair arrangements that, of course, I could not repeat myself. I have been fortunate always to have good hairdressers, both then in London, in Manchester and later when I moved to the Edinburgh area. My present one, Brian, tells me wicked stories as he dresses my hair. I had never had long hair before but decided in London to grow my hair. This was a new innovation for me but did not last long. Once in Manchester, I lost my chignon and reverted to short hair, which was much easier in theatre. It has remained short.

At the dinners, we always had a guest speaker, often a politician. Another yearly event was the pantomime produced by the junior staff. I was at various times Mary Whitehouse (with unruly children) or the woman who was delivered of an egg. The story was that I had been delivered of an egg instead of a child on a remote Scottish island. Due to the unusual circumstances, the egg and I were sent to GOS to be investigated, allowing each department to be involved.

Because of the unusual distribution of cases in London, it was decided that I needed to see the more common problems, and so I exchanged with a senior registrar in Edinburgh. Of course, it also meant that his experience improved. After three years, I was sent back to Scotland to the Hospital for Sick Children in Edinburgh. After having experienced (apart from older children) an average of six neonates a week, we had that number in six months! Life was much easier, and I could be out of the hospital when on call (with my bleep if needed). Our remit was to treat children up to age fifteen with general surgery and orthopaedic emergencies. There was at that time a senior registrar club for general surgical trainees who kindly invited me to join. They were all male except for one other female from Australia, doing breast surgery. One evening in my flat, we organised a dinner, doing the cooking ourselves—chicken marengo, jugged hare, and some dessert. The men were so impressed that they wanted us to do a meal every time, but we declined. I got to know many of the people I would meet again on my return to the Edinburgh College.

I enjoyed my time in Edinburgh, although not the emergency orthopaedics, despite getting a free Spanish meal after treating the son of the restaurant's owner, who had a fractured leg—so there were some compensations. On one occasion, while sitting at a desk in the doctors' room off the ward, my junior leant heavily on me, and the chair (a cantilever type) collapsed under our combined weight. Our boss at that time glanced into the room and said, "Big C." Whether it was me or my bust size, I never found out. I trained many of the juniors, and it could not have been too hard because one followed me back to GOS when I returned to London for a second time. Maybe it was my cooking—we used to cater for mess parties and even had a rather windy picnic at the top of Arthur's Seat.

After a very useful year, I returned to the professorial unit in London, now almost trained. To the surprise of our anaesthetist, Professor Wilkinson would let me operate unsupervised—unheard of before. He would of course comment on what I was doing. Around this time, I showed him the letter he had written in reply to mine asking for advice. We had the same letters after our names, and he was amused that he had disparaged my qualifications.

On going to a local bank one lunchtime, I rounded the corner and thought I was on a film set, but there were no cameras. Robbers were coming out of my bank. The general public was held back by the guns being pointed at us for real. After the robbers left, I ended up treating some of the employees who had had chemicals thrown in their face. The sister on the ward wondered why I had taken so long. She did not believe me until the incident was reported in the evening newspaper, and I received a huge bunch of flowers from the bank as thanks for my assistance.

Towards the end of my time, I did a locum consultant post in Queen Elizabeth Hospital, Hackney, and I also lectured on a British Council Course for doctors from overseas (trainees and general surgeons). The professor would always entertain them towards the end of the course. Both he and his wife were excellent hosts, and I tried to help. After they had all gone back to their residence, he was laying down the law about something, and his wife said, "Andrew, don't pontificate." He stopped! Some weekends we would go to Cambridge to operate on pigs (very similar guts to humans). This was to eventually help in gauging nutrition in

Enilorac

babies. One time I overslept, and after a flustered phone call, I was reassured by his wife, who told not to worry because he was not up yet either. We would wander round Cambridge, looking at the glorious colleges, before returning to London. A lasting friendship based on mutual respect lasted until his death. I was proud to do the eulogy at his funeral service.

While at GOS, I attended my first British Association of Paediatric Surgeons (BAPS) meeting in Genoa as a senior registrar. It happened that there was a hotel strike, and so we were all moved to Santa Marquerita, a lovely fishing town perched on the side of the beautiful blue Mediterranean Sea. At an evening reception, there were very few female toilets, and I cemented a lasting friendship with Gesine from Austria as we searched for one. This friendship lasted until her death from cancer of the breast. We even holiday together when we both arrived early in Greece before another BAPS meeting.

Old university friends appeared back in my life, and inevitably Ian, a pathologist then working in London, and I organised the first university reunion, as well as the second one in St Andrews. These were highly successful and have continued intermittently through the years. I did end up having to organise one in Manchester later.

On days off, I could visit Maidenhead, where I had two godchildren (offspring of one of the chaps who had demonstrated anatomy with me in Dundee). I became aware that one friend of the family had unhealthy interest in me when she wished to wash my car at GOS. I soon put a stop to this, much to my friend George's amusement. Over the years, I have had four godchildren. The others are the daughter of Humphrey (from my university year) and, much later, Ben (my secretary's son).

I had been awarded a certificate of completion of training in paediatric surgery from the College of Surgeons of Edinburgh at a diploma ceremony in June 1975. Now I required a permanent consultant post. At that time, there were not many posts in the UK, and although I had been offered one in the United States, I did not want to leave Britain. I kept applying.

9

Manchester and a Consultant Post

What Manchester says today, the rest of England says tomorrow.
Proverb

Mother and I went on holiday to Amsterdam, a lovely city with art galleries and museums and canal boats. We visited the Rikmuseum and the van Gogh museum. Then Mother suggested we visit a diamond factory which gave guided tours. Afterwards, she seemed interested in buying loose diamonds, much to my surprise. So of course, I got interested and eventually fell for a pinkie ring with two diamonds at a slant. Once I declared I was buying it, she lost interest in her diamonds. It had all been a ruse to get me to buy! How well she knew me. It became my lucky ring, and I have it still.

I had been called for interview for a senior lecturer and consultant post in paediatric surgery in Manchester. I could not afford to cancel the holiday and so flew to Manchester from Amsterdam, leaving Mother behind in the hotel. The hotel staff were very suspicious.

My referees were Wallace Dennison, the consultant who had tried to put me off by detailing all I would require; Professor Donald Douglas, my erstwhile boss (for junior jobs and research) and past president of Royal College of Surgeons of Edinburgh; and Professor Andrew Wilkinson, from GOS and also a past president of the Edinburgh College—an impressive lineup. Professor Wilkinson wished me the worst of British luck before I left because he wanted me to still be associated with his department and knew a post would soon be vacant in Hackney in London. Although I enjoyed my time in London, Manchester suited me better, being halfway between Scotland and London, with a catchment area at that time of four and a half million—loads of work to do.

The post was in one of the three academic general surgical departments with teaching and research responsibilities. A telling interview (held in the university) followed with the professor of psychiatry, Neil Kessels (who features later), suggesting that operating on handicapped children was a waste of time. He expected me to fold under his glare.

I had been well taught by Andrew Wilkinson and so was able to reply that helping the child to become well helped not only the child but also the parents. By making life a little easier for them, this was to the good. He then threw another googlie by asking why I would require lecture time, considering the bread-and-butter surgery was on the wards. My reply was that we needed some jam (information about the less common conditions) with the bread and butter. I got the job and returned to Mother the next day in high spirits.

Enilorac

I started in August 1975. Children's services in Manchester were spread all over the city. I would be mainly at Booth Hall Hospital in the north of the city (now a housing development), but I had emergency duties at Pendelbury Children's Hospital, situated in Salford, as well as at Duchess of York Hospital, a small children's hospital in the south. The surgical neonatal unit was just opening in the major maternity hospital at St Mary's, in the centre of the city next to Manchester Royal Infirmary, where incidentally the surgical department I was attached to was situated. With four hospitals to serve, I certainly needed a car (sadly, no longer a sports car) to get around, and initially a bleeper. I was very grateful when we were given mobile phones! I did (and still do) like to drive, which was just as well. Sometimes I would use a phrase that was met with blank looks—I had used a Scottishism and would have to rephrase it. I would annoy the "red roses" (Lancastrians) by saying I was doing missionary work in the North-West!

I was the third consultant for this large population; Ambrose Jolleys and Joe Cohen were my colleagues. When I retired, there were five consultants, and now I believe there are fourteen—nine practising paediatric surgery and five paediatric urologists! Although I had declared an interest in urology (having been trained by DI Williams in GOS), one of my colleagues was S. J. Cohen, a renowned and established paediatric urologist. We soon decided that he would take my urology cases, and I would take on his gastrointestinal cases.

I was fortunate that one of the paediatricians, Victor Miller, was keen to cooperate in this subspecialty. We established an endoscopy service for both upper and lower gastrointestinal tract, working amicably together. Diagnostic laparoscopy (and later operative technique) was slow in being used in children, and I was one of the first to use this diagnostic addition some years later. We also collaborated on biliary atresia cases, where the liver cannot drain into the bowel, leading to liver damage. Morio Kasai, a Japanese paediatric surgeon, had recently developed an operation which in some cases could help. The results were not marvellous, but at that time one-third of the patients could be helped; otherwise, they all died.

My first medical staff meeting (three weeks after starting work) was interesting. Although there was a locum female neurosurgeon, Carys Bannister, there was no established female consultant in the hospital, never mind a female surgeon! The chairman, a well-established paediatrician, attempted to railroad the closure of half the surgical beds and then move rapidly on to the next item on the agenda. I interrupted by pointing out my plans for developing gastrointestinal services with the help of Victor Miller by establishing endoscopy, and that I would require beds for this. It shut him up, and for the time being I retained the beds. The icing on the cake was a note passed across the boardroom table from an orthopaedic surgeon whom I already knew was difficult: "Please, may I always fight on your side." I had arrived. I knew that if I did not set out my patch, I would forever be on the back foot. Throughout my consultant life, no one ever tried to do that again without good reason.

The district administrator arranged for Irene, then very new and just out of college, to be my secretary because I was the new consultant. We developed a modus operandi between us. She remained my secretary throughout my consultant life and is a very close friend; I am godmother to her son. She was greatly helped initially by Joe Cohen's secretary. Joe and I had rooms off a bigger room, where the secretaries sat. Judith, Joe's secretary, was well established and could show Irene the ropes. By starting together, Irene and I became a formidable pair walking down the corridor together to clinic, because both of us were very tall. Parents knew they could phone and ask for advice, and if necessary, the message would be passed on to me. We worked well together, organising operating lists and the waiting list with total control in our hands. She is now in charge of all the secretaries. The same district administrator (one of the good ones) who gave me Irene was reassuring when I got on the Edinburgh College Council because it would involved time away. He said it reflected well on Manchester and the hospitals. When I retired, the person I missed most was Irene.

Because of the shared office space, Joe and I developed a marvellous working relationship. We did not always agree, but we never parted in anger. The doors to our offices were always open unless we were consulting with patients and parents.

Initially, I stayed in a house belonging to the hospital just down the road. When Mother came to inspect it, we cleaned it up. At the end of her holiday, I took her to the station to get a train north to Edinburgh and thence to Dundee with a taxi to Forfar (thanks to Beecham's cuts, now without a station). I told her not to move. After I left, they were told to change trains to go to York because there was trouble with the west coast line! She almost missed her connection north. As so often happens, comments were made by the other passengers in the compartment, which made for a reasonably pleasant journey for her. When I phoned in the evening to check on her safe arrival home, I got no answer and was worried. I kept phoning but made no contact, and so when she eventually phoned, the telephonist told her I was worried and that she was glad Mother was okay. Mother then regaled me with the details of her awful journey. One of the other passengers said he was called Walter Scott!

Once, a porter appeared at my front door to check I was okay. I had had a bath, and the anglepoise lamp had fallen on the phone set, melting it and fusing the handset to the base. Talk about a hotline! These are illustrations of the kind of people I was working with in Manchester.

Via a general practitioner who referred a patient to me, I finally bought a townhouse (with a sauna) halfway between Booth Hall and Pendelbury, with reasonable access to the city centre and St Mary's Hospital. It was in a very Jewish area, and so shops were open on Sunday. I used to say that I lived halfway between a prison (Strangeways) and a mental hospital (Prestwich used to be such in North Manchester) and let people decide which was more appropriate. Mother had retired and had no ties to Forfar, and so she moved to Manchester, bringing her furniture with her. For a time, she was my "housekeeper". When she became more disabled, we finally moved a few doors away to a semi-detached house with a garden. She no longer was able to garden, and I took over and found that I enjoyed it. While she was still able-bodied, we went to a car show (the first and only time), and I bought the car she fell in love with: a sleek Honda

Prelude that we called Olga (the registration was KDB). Eventually this had to be changed for a car that would take the wheelchair because she was unable to walk far.

Initially, the only way the hospitals could contact me if I was not at home was by the use of bleepers, which would go off at the most inappropriate times with no phone in easy reach. When you were driving, you never knew which hospital wanted you. Late at night while returning home from operating on a newborn baby, I had to decide whether I would continue home, return to St Mary's (where the babies were), or go to Booth Hall. Or it could have been the two other hospitals scattered around Manchester. On one occasion while driving to a meeting in Liverpool, I suffered a puncture, which I had to change the wheel myself with difficulty. My bleep kept going, and of course I could not answer it. By the time I reached Liverpool University, I was tired, irritable, and dirty. When the poor junior doctor at the other end of the phone said, "I just wanted to tell you …" I said, "Don't you just me!" Poor lad. It became so much easier with mobile phones, but no less busy. Again, at night I was returning home when my car broke down near a pub in a not very salubrious area. I was able to phone the AA and get help without leaving the car.

Every year, the hospital put on a pantomime, and because I had been involved in GOS, of course I became involved. One of the theatre sisters who often worked with me, Teresa, was very small, and we would do a routine. One year we did Snow White and the seven dwarves. I, of course, was Doc, and Irene was Sleepy. Who said that dwarves were small?

When working on a case, I considered myself as having three patients, the child and the parents. The child was the most important. I would draw (not very well) what was wrong and how I intended to correct the problem. For example, when explaining to the parents of a newborn baby who was suffering from a blockage of the stomach exit (duodenal atresia), my drawing showed how I would bypass the problem. The father, who was a plumber, immediately understood what I was going to do.

I made a point of gaining the confidence of the children by not appearing as a strange, white-coated figure. Ward rounds were often done with a toddler on my hip. If I was on the ward at lunchtime, the children loved it when I pinched a chip from the lunch trolley. If I had time, I would play with them and tease the boys as to which football team was which.

I taught students and nurses about paediatric surgery—the common and the uncommon. The students were all from Manchester University, but some had started out at my old university, St Andrews. By this time, only a medical science degree was possible in St Andrews which had no clinical facilities. A Vice Chancellor of Manchester University and a former St Andrews graduate arranged that these students could come to Manchester if they wished, or they could go elsewhere. Although some of the teaching was in tutorial and lecture format, I also taught on the wards, in the theatre, and in outpatients. I enjoyed this immensely, and think I did well—if the feedback was honest.

Victor Miller was a gastrointestinal paediatrician, and when we were doing endoscopy worked well together, he was the only physician who worked in theatre. As well as collaborating on this and biliary atresia, we also combined our resources to look after children with inflammatory bowel disease (IBD). One such child, a twelve-year-old, required intravenous feeding before urgent emergency surgery. When I saw him the day before surgery, he remarked on what wonderful stuff the feeding was. He had grown hairs on his chest, put there by himself from his comb. He required a total removal of his large bowel and a permanent stoma. At follow-up, the only problem was that the rest of the class at school wanted a stoma too! Many years later, when lecturing to the medical students on IBD and the need sometimes for such stomas, at least one of the class was listening. He looked like the front row forward of a rugby team, and I did not recognise him as the same boy until he said his name. He agreed with what I had been teaching and became a GP in the area.

Another service I established was a constipation clinic for children. This was run in conjunction with district nurses, and it proved to be very helpful. Most patients simply needed advice about diet and occasionally medicine. However, some had more serious problems which were picked up earlier. Because of my interest in lower bowel problems, I became known as "the bum lady of the North -West"!

Despite being a university appointment, I did very little research, rather concentrating on the teaching aspect. Investigation into oesophageal and also anal pressures was carried out, as well as work on diaphragmatic hernias. Most research work was helping facilitate things for others—consultants and trainees doing their research. I had little inclination to do research, let alone time for it, especially once I was involved in medical politics.

We were one of the first units to perform regular endoscopy sessions, and so Victor and I ran endoscopy courses with our radiologist in 1991. I was involved in British Council courses for neonatal and paediatric surgery in Liverpool, and I organised one in Manchester. These were for trainees from abroad. Such British Council courses in 1991, 1993, and 1998 led to me being on their committee in London. The courses also extended my influence to Europe (e.g., Poland) and further afield. Some of the participants are still in contact with me.

As indicated before, I had numerous hospitals to attend. My base was Booth Hall Hospital, where my routine surgery and outpatients were held. However, I would be on call for emergencies for Pendlebury Children's hospital and the neonates at St Mary's Hospital in the centre of the city. We also did emergency cover for the Duchess of York Hospital, a small children's hospital in the south of the city. It had been started by a woman paediatrician. This meant I would be working in Booth Hall, requiring to deal with a neonatal emergency operation at St Mary's at the same time as an emergency case at Duchess of York—as happened on one occasion.

This was obviously untenable, and along with others, I campaigned to have the Duchess hospital closed. This was considered dreadful, and questions were even asked in parliament at Westminster. Started by a woman, and now a woman trying to close it! All investigations had to be carried out in an adult hospital farther south. Some years later, the Duchess of York hospital was closed and moved to the adult hospital farther south. Because of all the travelling, my car was a necessity and I got to know all the back routes around Manchester—a necessity to avoid busy main roads so that I could reach my destination as quickly as I could.

Because of the various hospitals, over the years I was on numerous committees. The chairman of one remarked I had been unusually quiet; usually I had positive suggestions to make on the matters under discussion. I remarked I had nothing to say—there was no use in speaking just for the sake of being heard. Later, I was on the Awards committee for the region, but the committee I enjoyed most was the Admissions committee for the university, helping to decide on candidates for medical school.

Professor Kessels (of my original interview) requested that I take part in a lunchtime discussion group of senior students as a female role model. He gave me lunch and warned me that the audience would be small, so I should not be too disappointed. The room was packed, and we had an interesting hour.

In the eighties, I was interviewed for a couple of articles on Women in Medicine and their problems. In the nineties, I was approached to write a short book on baby hernias aimed at adult surgeons. I also wrote numerous chapters for major volumes on gastrointestinal problems in children: biliary atresia, inflammatory bowel disease, Hirshsprung's disease, and atresias (absence) of the small and large bowel. Numerous papers on this and more mundane aspects of children's surgery followed either written or presented at conferences.

Look North the local TV programme, ran a series called "A Day in the Life of …", and I was featured. It meant having a film crew with me for a whole day in theatre, on the wards, and in outpatients. My morning ward round (before theatre) caused problems because I walked too fast into the ward, and it had to be repeated several times before it was caught on camera. However, it went down well—even though one of the senior nurses did not approve of me saying, "I cut up little children but make them better." But it was true.

I organised a Spring meeting of the Edinburgh College of Surgeons which was held in 1987 with me and a committee of two others: the urologist I had first met when we'd both failed the fellowship in London, and a dentist. A committee of three—perfect! Mother helped too. Over the years, I gave certain prestigious lectures as president of various societies and associations. In 1988, I gave the Mason Brown lecture (on Inflammatory Bowel Disease in Childhood) in Edinburgh at the college.

Our middle-grade trainees were general surgical registrars wanting paediatric experience (at that time, some general surgeons operated on children but not on babies) or paediatric surgical registrars. Many of the consultant surgeons in the north-west spent some time with me. One of them, an Irishman called Leo, had a very rickety car. Once while taking me and Irene, my secretary, to collect my car (which was being serviced), the windscreen wipers on his car failed. He put his hand out his window to keep them going! Then he ran out of petrol. None of us had any money, and so he charmed a passer-by to lend him some so he could phone his wife. Needless to say, we did not travel with him again. Over the years, on top of British council courses, we attracted overseas trainees from El Salvador, Malaysia, India, Nepal, and Kenya. This last was particularly close to my heart because Daddy had been there during the war. I ended up saying I was the mother of paediatric surgery in Kenya because at one time, I had trained all such surgeons except the professor. We also had trainees from Lebanon, Singapore, and Malawi, leading to lasting friendships.

Working in a children's hospital was not without incident, although when the IRA bomb went off in the centre of Manchester, we were on standby but not involved. One Boxing Day, I saw a squirrel (a frequent pest) at our bird table, and so I stepped out in my dressing gown to scare him off. Unfortunately, it had been raining on top of ice, and I went flat on my back on the patio and broke my left wrist. He metaphorically thumbed his nose at me. I drove to my hospital, a children's one, and casualty requested the senior registrar attend, only saying that I was there. He was angry with them for having called me before him—until he saw my wrist. I was in a plaster for six weeks, and I was helped afterwards by an excellent physiotherapist to return to operating. She knew me well because she was already helping me with my then occasional back problems, employing acupuncture. Some years later, after having visited a patient in a ward, I was returning to my office when I fell again, this time on a wet floor which had been left by the cleaner. I broke my right wrist, which required manipulation under anaesthetic. Irene's mother helped me (by this time Mummy had died) and stayed with me, even helping me to bathe. The consultant who dealt with me at Booth Hall when my three juniors came to see what had happened was surprised, especially when I said this was my family—a Muslim, a Hindu, and a Sikh girl.

It was unfortunate that I was travelling to East Africa shortly afterwards, with my arm in plaster. I started in Kenya, and my former trainees insisted I visit them if I was in Africa. I had a great time meeting people in different areas of work, including lawyers and civil servants. I was shown round by my first trainee, Peter, who introduced me as his mentor to his senior nurse. She replied that she considered him her mentor, which made me her grandmother!

Because paediatric surgery is a small speciality—there were at that time fewer than one hundred in UK—we had connections worldwide. This allowed for an easy exchange of ideas and trainees. Most of my junior doctors were excellent, and I am glad to say that some of the women have continued in general surgery, orthopaedic, and paediatric surgery.

Two local male graduates were good but were quite cheeky to some of my registrar and nursing staff. It was decided by all departments to teach them a lesson—with my help. A scenario was played out in the X-ray department, which was close to a road between the hospital wards. Supposedly I had been knocked down and was semiconscious with a fractured femur. The radiology department even managed to produce an X-ray of a fractured femur with my name on it. The two doctors were called to their consultant—other middle-grade staff being conveniently busy elsewhere. The casualty nursing staff were amazingly not as helpful as usual, and these two were becoming very anxious. I was a contact lens wearer (and had taken them out), and so they could touch my eyes without me flinching. I even allowed them to feel for the femoral pulse on my supposedly injured leg. At last I sat up, and every one fell about, laughing at their discomfort. What I had not expected was that the story of this prank got to Manchester Royal Infirmary, and I got a rude reaction from Rory, one of my general surgical colleagues in the academic department.

Enilorac

After Mother's death, a group of my trainees and I would have suppers at my home. I rather suspect Ram (the Hindu) thought I was not feeding myself. If none of us was on call, on the spur of the moment, an evening would be arranged. We took it in turns to do the cooking, one would be in charge, and the others did the shopping and assisting. We would include visiting medics and Irene. I insisted that in the kitchen, I was Caroline, although at least one of them had problems with that. A visiting female Indian doctor annoyed Ram (who was in charge) by lifting lids and generally bothering him. She was horrified when he told me to cut the tomatoes smaller—I was his consultant boss! She was not invited back. When Navid was in charge, he had to keep phoning his wife for instructions, but his tomato salad was superb. Ram and his wife have remained friends with me, and we visit once a year and are always in contact.

Another mutual leisure activity was attending a "Colour Me Beautiful" evening run by one of the ward assistants. This was with two other female doctors: a senior house officer who had been a medical missionary doctor in Africa, and the registrar on rotation from general surgery. Irene was also involved. Each of us was found to be a different season. Despite (or perhaps because of) the fact the organiser had said that very few people were able to wear black, I wore a knitted black frock. I turned out to be winter, the only one who should wear black, so I was wearing the right colour. I also became a member of the Wine Society, which unfortunately I cannot enjoy so much now because of medication.

During my training and all of my working life, I wore high-heeled shoes—even two inches on one occasion—so I really did look down on people. On one notable occasion, I was helping a general surgical colleague to canvas for political office, and to his disgust, I patted him on the head; he was already small in stature. Clothes were important because I liked to buy nice things which suited me, but more important, I felt it gave a good professional impression. I would say I must have masculine tendencies to be a successful surgeon, but all my professional life, I did try to maintain my femininity, liking clothes and jewellery.

Every year the British Association of Paediatric Surgeons held a meeting, with every three years being in the United Kingdom and Europe. Manchester was host in 1993, but because I was involved in a British Council course at the time, my colleagues did the organising. As well as the BAPS meetings, I regularly attended the Hungarian Paediatric Surgeons meetings. The first held in Pecs led to an interesting journey. My plane into Budapest was late, and so I missed my train connection. At that time, Hungary was still communist, so no beds could be had in Budapest (without a backhander), and so eventually I travelled two hundred kilometres south by taxi—and it only cost me the equivalent of twenty pounds. Friends I made then are still part of my life. A joke we were told while there involved all three heads of state from Russia, United States, and Hungary travelling in a car. The chauffeur asked Gorbachev which way to turn. "Left, of course." Then it was Reagan's turn. He replied, "Right." By the time it was the Hungarian's turn, he said, "Indicate left, but turn right"—a true depiction of what Hungary thought at that time.

Enilorac

I was asked to chair a session in Dresden—an even more repressive regime. This I did with Andrew, my friend from Pecs. My German was poor, but sometimes even he did not know the words even in Hungarian. Somehow we managed. The locals would look at the wall and say, "What shall we tell them?"

One case stands out in my memory: a road traffic accident in Manchester involving a young boy. He was seriously ill and bleeding, and they immediately took him to the only theatre available in the late afternoon. As people became available, they arrived to help; this included other consultants in different specialties, even if they had officially finished work. Sadly, the outcome was not good.

I was involved in the Manchester Medical Society, especially the paediatric and surgical sections, and was president of the paediatric section from 1999 to 2000 and the surgical section from 1998 to 1999. There were three other female consultant surgeons in the area: the neurosurgeon (already mentioned) and two general surgeons, one a member of the Medical Womens federation(MWF) and also of the English College's senior group. I was a council member of the paediatric section of the Royal Society of Medicine in London (1984–1987), and by the time of my retirement, I was president of the NW Surgeons Association. However, my involvement stretched beyond Manchester and its environs, making me known throughout the northwest even though I was in a small specialty. I also became a Soroptimist (like the Rotary club), which was an excellent way to mix with nonmedical women. When Mother was ill, I was allowed a sabbatical, and after she died they were very helpful. When I moved to Edinburgh, they passed my name on so contact could be made. Interestingly, my cousin Jennifer was a leading light in her region, and Helen (from schooldays) was at one time national president of the Soroptimists.

Near the end of my time in Manchester, we were required to go on an assertive course. My secretary fell about laughing. I certainly did not require that, never being unwilling to put my head above the parapet. As well as being busy clinically (only three surgeons then, with no split off of urology), we were on call for a week at a time. We had connections with Alder Hey Children's Hospital in Liverpool, despite the M62 being considered the big divide (like between Glasgow and Edinburgh).Various committees for the university (Admissions committee for ten years) and a working party looking at assessing academic departments kept me busy, to say nothing of the NHS committees (e.g., paediatric surgical training in the north-west and being a training advisor). I was the role model I never had. As well as being on staff committees in Booth Hall and St Mary's, I was on general surgical committees in North Manchester, Central, and Withington Hospital in the South. Like my maternal grandfather, I was always going to a meeting!

Many trainees passed through my hands, some intent on paediatric surgery and others merely expanding their general surgical training. My influence is far-reaching in Britain and overseas. Samir from Lebanon, Rang, a Kurd, and Edward from Malawi were initially very wary of each other, but they soon became sound friends. Sadly, Edward could not return to Malawi and ended up in Liverpool as a consultant in emergency medicine, dying far too young. Samir once remarked one could not see Edward in the dark unless he smiled, and there were laughs all round. Samir is still in my life and features later. Another close friend who started off as a trainee was "little" Carolyn from Singapore. She did excellent research into biliary atresia before returning home to eventually head the department. She was a friend to both me and Mother.

I did not like public speaking, but I did give an address to local BMA groups, and once I replied to the Lassies at a Burns night supper. I think many of my colleagues considered me a BDW—a bloody difficult woman—but there usually was a very good reason. Although I had a superb relationship with Joe Cohen, I cannot say the same for my colleagues when I retired; only one has kept in contact, and he is considered a difficult Scot too. He had been one of my trainees before becoming a consultant.

During my time in Manchester, two family deaths occurred: Uncle Sandy (father's brother) in 1983, and Alan (Mother's brother) in 1985. It is a pity that Uncle Sandy never knew of my successful career in medical politics. Alan tried to make much of it, to Mother's disgust. He kept phoning up to speak to her, and she eventually got me to do the talking!

Children are much better patients than adults because they do not pretend—they are either well or ill. They also bounce back quickly after surgery. Also, most of them are not fat, and very few die unless one deals with cancer patients (which I did not). I had no children of my own but tried (not always successfully) to not have favourites. I did enjoy working with children. It is rewarding, knowing that you have made it possible for a child to lead a normal life.

As a surgeon, one must make decisions quickly, and they are not always easy. My nurses and juniors knew that if they were lazy, they would get the rough edge of my tongue. However, if they did well, I would praise them to the skies. The theatre staff I worked with were superb. We worked as a team both in theatre and on the wards, which was very important. Along with Irene, my secretary, this was why I think the children and their parents were well looked after. Since I have retired, two former patients, now healthy adults, have been in contact to say hi! The thing I missed most on retirement was this important working in a team, as well as Irene to write my letters. There were no role models for me when I started out, but throughout my working life, I acted as such for many girls who came to me for advice—and perhaps more who had became aware of the existence of a female surgeon.

!st Dance at Forfar Academy

Tom sitting on my knee at university

Mother and Jane at my 21st Birthday party in Forfar

My first car- a black and white Triumph Herald

Rag Day in Dundee- Edna and I as Heavenly Twins

Graduation photograph

With the lads in Yorkhill Childrens Hospital

My Bond Eguipe sports car

Professor AW Wilkinson and me in the ward in GOS

Booth Hall Hospital

Irene (my secretary) with British Council students and me

In my Theatre being filmed for TV

First lady on Council of Royal College of Surgeons of Edinburgh (Glasgow Herald photograph)

Presenting the Hunter-Doig Medal in my dark and light blue college gown in the College

Official College photograph on being elected to Council

Some of my committee at General Medical Council with Johanna on the left

10

Medical Politics

All the world's a stage, and all the men and women merely players............and one man in his time plays many parts.
—William Shakespeare *As you like it*

Ever since I was a junior doctor, I had been a member of the Medical Women's Federation (MWF), established in the early twentieth century to support equal rights for women doctors in the workplace. A professor in gynaecology in Dundee had introduced me to the local branch. However, over the years, whilst remaining a member, I rarely had time to go to the meetings in Dundee, Durham, Glasgow, or London. Once established in Manchester, I did attend meetings and become more active. In time, I was voted to the council, which met in the headquarters in Tavistock Square, London. I became local president in Manchester and in due course national president in 1985. At the same time, I was elected onto the Council of the Royal College of Surgeons of Edinburgh. I took up my presidency in

Enilorac

Cambridge, giving an address titled "The Hands of a Lady". At the dinner the evening before this, as the top table was about to process in, one of the local organisers suddenly said that I would be giving the benediction before the meal. Having been caught unaware, I gave them the Selkirk toast from Burns in broad Scots!

Being president of the MWF involved mountains of paperwork and meetings in London, as well as meeting with other bodies (e.g., the Royal College of Surgeons of England and the Obstetric College in Regent's Park). One had to give lectures, attend official dinners, and chair twice yearly meetings of the federation. One of the dinners in the Obstetric College was hosted by their president, Narin Patel, who had done my student locums for me when I was a junior—what a small world. At that time, final year medical students would get more experience by standing in for junior house officers when they went on holiday. The Medical Women's Federation meetings were held in London in the winter, but they were hosted by local associations around the country, even in Belfast during the Troubles. I helped to revive the Manchester group, which had been among the first to start the federation. When I became past president, Mummy remarked that there was nothing so past as a past president. The huge amount of mail suddenly stopped; the Internet was not yet in common use. As well as organising a Manchester meeting, once I retired I organised a national meeting in Edinburgh in the College of Surgeons. In retirement, I became president of the Edinburgh group too.

Although I attended Edinburgh and English Colleges meetings, I was not initially too involved with them. I became an examiner in the Edinburgh College in 1980, especially liking to examine in anatomy, pathology, principles of surgery, and operative surgery. Initially, this was just for the Primary examination. I had the odd experience of examining in anatomy with Rex Coupland who had been the professor of anatomy in Dundee during my time there. I liked the subject and think I did okay. In 1982 I progressed to the full fellowship examination, which involved applied physiology, pathology, and operative surgery, as well as clinical cases in a hospital setting. On one occasion, I examined in the clinical fellowship in Dundee with one of my old bosses, W. F. Walker. It was a great experience examining with him on my old ward. He had tried to dissuade me from surgery and then helped a great deal by arranging a meeting with A. A. Wilkinson, which ultimately led to the post in Great Ormond Street Hospital.

These two men from my past, Willie Walker (then a council member) and Andrew Wilkinson (an ex-president), together and separately persuaded me to stand for the Council of the Edinburgh College of Surgeons. A female member of council was unheard of since the college had started, in 1505 (the oldest of these colleges). I was in a very small speciality and had never examined abroad (a large number of the fellows of the Edinburgh college come from overseas). It was unlikely that I would be successful—but it would stop these two from pestering me. However, my involvement in the NW Surgical scene and membership of the British Surgical Association, at which meetings I was "that tall Scottish female paediatric surgeon", meant I was well known.

In 1984 I got elected to the Council nearly stopping Willie Walker from returning to council. I was one of fifteen candidates for five places. I had made medical history, even

Enilorac

if it had taken women four hundred years. It was sixty-four years since a woman had got the fellowship in 1920—Alice Headward (later Hunter), who worked in India. In 1984 the number of women fellows on the college roll had gone up to 252, as compared to less than 100 when I got my fellowship. Eleanor Davies-Colley was the first woman in the English College to get her fellowship in 1911, and so we were behind the times. There was at that time a woman on the council of the English College who kindly sent me a letter of congratulations.

The other council members and the then president, Sir James Fraser, seemed delighted with their first lady, lining up at my first meeting to kiss me. Mother was at that first dinner, and after I was installed, she remarked to Sir James that they might rue the day!

Shortly after my election, the college held an out-of-town meeting in Oxford. An old gentleman approached me, and after stating his connection with the college, he looked me up and down, nodded, and said, "I voted for you." Apparently I passed muster. My election was unique and was featured in various Scottish papers: *Dundee Courier*, *Scotsman,* and on the front page of the *Glasgow Herald,* with a picture. This caused consternation to one of my Manchester colleagues when he spied it on the news stand. I was required to have photographs for various publications—not something I liked having done. In the millennium the college commissioned a photograph of the council to mimic a painting done in 1900, which of course had no women present. I was the only member of council to have a pocket in my ceremonial gown. I could not carry a handbag, and so the college officer, Mr Walker, sewed one in for me.

This appointment involved even more work. Apart from monthly meetings of Council in Edinburgh, I was on various subcommittees. This was all when I was also president of the Medical Women's Federation. Now I had the triangle of Manchester, London, and Edinburgh to travel in various combinations. When in Edinburgh, I would stay in the George Hotel, where Mother had spent her first night as a married lady. Later, when Mother became ill, I would drive up to Edinburgh from Manchester in the early morning and then return in the evening—very tiring. I remained on the council for five years and then was re-elected for a further five years. Then it was necessary to be off council for two years before again being successful in the elections in 1996. By the end of my third term, I was retired and felt that fifteen years was enough, so I did not stand again. During my time on Council, we had a few combined meetings with the English College of Surgeons. This led to better understanding of each other, albeit for a short period of time. I got to know other surgeons and met old friends.

At the same time, once retired, I felt it was inappropriate to continue to give legal opinions because one quickly gets out of date. Throughout my career, I did many legal cases, giving professional advice. I never had to appear in court and was glad to give it up. I continued for a short time to examine for the college, but only as a nonmedical person.

As a college, we have strong connections overseas, and this involved travel to examine, have meetings, and attend conferences around the world. Travel overseas was hard work, examining almost every day and then being entertained at night, but I enjoyed meeting doctors from different cultures and in different specialties. Singapore, Kuala Lumpur, and

Enilorac

Hong Kong were my main destinations, with over ten times in both Singapore and Hong Kong. It was thought it would be difficult for all parties if I examined in Saudi Arabia. I was on Council for three terms, and presidents came and went: Sir Ian Fraser (who had also examined me in my final fellowship clinical), Professor Geoffry Chisholm, Professor Paddy Boulter, Arnold Maran, Sir Robert Shields, and Sir John Temple (who had been in Salford when I had started at Manchester).

As council members, we were required to serve on various committees. Initially I served on Science and Education(for three terms) Development, Nominations and Finance. As well as being a member of the Speciality Advisory Board, I became chairman for four years in 1989. On my retirement, once I was off council, I briefly became Director of Heritage before we appointed a trained museum director. This department has interviewed me on tape for the archives, and at the moment it has the video running continuously in the museum!

I was delighted to note that when I retired from the council in 2001, the number of female fellows had increased to 1,451, up from 252 at the time I had got on council. Although I never held office (standing for vice president once), I have been followed by more women in the intervening years. There has always been at least one woman on council, and at present there are six women on council, one being an office bearer, and 2,042 of the fellows are women (9 per cent). I helped set up the Ladies group of the college for female surgeons, as well as wives and widows of surgeons, so that they could remain part of the college. It involved meetings and occasional outings, such as to

Abbotsford. Sadly, this is now dissolving. I now attend the senior group in the college, which involves retired surgeons, anaesthetists, and dentists. It meets once a month except in the summer for a lecture (not necessarily medical) and lunch. It is good to still be part of it, and I enjoy meeting old friends.

Other activities involving the college was the Mason Brown lecture in 1988 on "Inflammatory Bowel Disease in Childhood", organised by the College and the British Association of Paediatric Surgeons. I also did a Christmas children's lecture, "Cornelia's Jewels—Her Children", about some conditions in childhood that could be made better by surgery. Very few of the children had to leave the room!

I never examined or stood for council of the English College, but I was part of Women in Surgical Training,(WIST) which started in 1991 from that college. The Edinburgh College followed a year later with an advisor for women surgeons. I joined Avril Mansfield, an English college council member, at the beginning of WIST. We first met when I gave a paper to the Surgical Research Society. Despite her seniority, she was good to this very junior female colleague. We are the only two members of the Tall Women's Surgical Club!

Once retired, I was elected to the committee for the senior surgeons of the English College, which meets twice a year: in London in the winter, and elsewhere in the country in the summer. With Ian MacLaren, a close friend and fellow ex-council member, I helped organise a successful combined meeting of the two seniors groups in Edinburgh. At these meetings, I renew old friendships within the general surgical field.

Enilorac

I have endowed and made provision in my will for a Doig-Hunter medal, which will be given intermittently by the Edinburgh College to a junior female consultant surgeon. She must be one who people think will make her mark. "As long as I am still presentable," said by one of my college friends, "I can present it." Alice Headward Hunter was the first woman to pass the Edinburgh fellowship in 1920, but she did not take her seat because she was a missionary in India. The first to do so in the same year was Gertrude Hertzfeld, who became a paediatric surgeon in Edinburgh. I still get invited to various college functions and dinners. There exists a photograph of me in my gown in the college shortly after making history. I managed to take part in the five-hundred-year celebrations of the College of Surgeons of Edinburgh with a procession to Greyfriars Churchyard, where many eminent surgeons had been buried in the past.

While I was still working, Alan Parks, then president of the English College, invited me as his personal guest to a dinner in London. I was on the council of the Edinburgh college, and this caused a few raised eyebrows. But I was amongst friends and had a splendid evening, even being seen back to my club in London.

While still on the Edinburgh council, I attended an overseas meeting of the English College in Barbados and the United States in 2001. Barbados was lovely, and two research fellows asked me to help them with their presentations. They were so grateful that they wished to repay me—by taking me out on a jet ski! Despite my demurring, we did go, with a Mae West to ensure safety. Mine did not quite meet because I am well endowed. I had my arms round one fellow's waist, which was okay until the other came too close. I fell off, and it is very difficult to get back on board from water. They both stopped and tried to help, and soon we were all in the water. I ended up saying, "I don't care where you put your hands—just get me back on board!" They both became very worried about this old lady. I was not worried because I am a strong swimmer. I knew that because we had hired the jet skis, the local Barbadians would come looking for us, which they did. He said to flop so that he could get me into his boat, which I did. By this time, there was an audience on the beach, and it looked as if I was a dead body. The sigh of relief from one of the senior people from the English College was audible as I walked up the beach. I asked him what the problem was. The two colleges at that time were not talking to each other, and he was worried as to how he would tell the Edinburgh College that they, the English Council, had killed one of their council members! Apart from an aching chest muscle for some time, I was okay.

At one of the national meetings of the Medical Women's Federation, two friends approached me and pointed out that elections for the General Medical Council (GMC) were imminent. I said, "So?" They continued. "We need more women on the GMC." Then they added, "We need more women from the north-west of the country." It became obvious what they wanted me to do. It was easier to give in to their persuasion, and it was highly unlikely that I would be successful—again, a small speciality.

However, at my first attempt in 1989, I was elected to the GMC, and later again in 1994 and 1999 The meetings, then held in Hallam Street, London, were very large at that time with elected, appointed members (from universities and colleges) and lay members, so I was content to sit at the back and learn. Others had different ideas, and I was elected to the overseas committee, chaired at that time by Professor Neil Kessels from Manchester. In 1994, I became chairman of the Overseas Registration Committee—the first woman to be a chairman of a major committee in the GMC. This meant sitting at the top table with other chairmen. By now, two other women have been included: Beulah Bewely (Finance) and Thelma Bates (Health). One of them had been one of the instigators in getting me on the GMC.

The uniqueness is illustrated by two incidents. When the president read out the names of chairmen, a certain doctor stood up and started to bemoan the lack of women and overseas doctors as chairmen. The president's reply was, "I've just mentioned Miss Doig. I think she is a woman!" The other involved a question from the floor to "Madam Chair". At this point, I stopped him and remarked that I was not a piece of furniture, but a chairman. Later, I became a member and then chairman of the Assessment Referral Committee. I was a member of the President's Advisory Committee. I served under Sir Robert Kilpatrick, a delightful and efficient man from Edinburgh, and I kept meeting him after retirement. I also had Sir Donald Irvine and Professor Graham Catto as presidents. Unfortunately, my directness and loathing of waffle got some people's backs up, and so I did not renew my involvement with the GMC.

Being on so many committees necessitated staying in London, and so I became a member of a club. I was a member of the Lansdowne Club off Berkley Square. Women are treated as equal members, and there is a full-sized swimming pool in the basement, which suited me well.

The dining room was also excellent. Through the GMC, I made another close friend, Johanna, a lay member of my committee. My involvement in the college and the GMC allowed me to slowly withdraw from medical life when I retired without it being too sudden a step. I was then ready for my third life.

Despite having made history in the Edinburgh College and the General Medical Council, I was never ambitious, only wanting to first become a doctor and then a surgeon. I certainly would not have believed people if they had predicted the outcome.

11

Travel

Travel broadens the mind but you must have the mind.
—G. K. Chesterton *The Shadow of the Shark*

One of my pleasures is meeting new people and travelling. Initially, Mother and I had little spare cash, and so holidays involved Arbroath on the east coast of Scotland, staying with my grandparents, or Cullen on the Moray Firth, staying with relatives of my maternal grandmother. It was only after I was earning that we could have holidays abroad. I was also fortunate that through examining and clinical work, I was required to travel.

Our first trip overseas was to Copenhagen. We stayed in a hotel just off the Radhus Platz and visited all the sights. One day, we sat in a boat on a canal as part of a tour that had not yet started. We were in the pouring rain, much to the amusement of passers-by. We were on water and might as well get wet too! A British Council trainee doctor, Inge, lived in the city and took us up to the north of the island.

She also took us to a circus, much to Mother's displeasure. We both loved the city and the smell of cigars.

When I was in Durham, we sailed via Newcastle to Oslo on a Fred Olsen ship. Imbalance following her mastoid operation meant that Mummy was naturally unsteady, and the rough seas at the mouth of the Tyne River did not upset her; she was one of very few in the dining room the first night. I was not one of them. One morning when we were joined by the others at a table for six, she remarked about the grass-covered roofs. I told her that we were not talking about them. Her reply was "No? But I am!" Unfortunately, one of the men at our table took a shine to her (she was still a good-looking woman) and had to be told by her to return to his wife.

A car journey round Ireland (both north and south) finished up in Dublin, a great city. I was mistaken for a man in Belfast because I was tall and wearing a trench coat, and the receptionist did not look up. The hotel we were originally booked into at Glengariff in the south was not great, but we found one down by the water's edge with a sign telling us to beware of twins and turkeys; more on this later. In Dublin, which we both loved, we discovered Jammet's, a restaurant run by two French brothers that is sadly no more. The food was superb and the service was delightful. It was during this holiday that I started to have problems with urinary tract infection. On returning to Dundee, I had an intravenous pyelogram,(IVP) which showed bilateral duplex kidneys and a scoliosis of the lumbar spine. The kidneys did not necessarily cause me problems, but my back has limited my activities as I got older. I was too old in my thirties to have any treatment, and at that time it was not noticeable.

Enilorac

The X-rays with two abnormalities were excellent teaching material when I was in Manchester.

Paris was another short break. We both loved rivers and food, and so it suited us well. We found a delightful little restaurant near the hotel that was frequented by the French. It was full early on in the evening with Parisians. Sitting next to us was a group of middle-aged French men, one of whom asked permission to smoke. Mother replied it was no problem and that it was nice to be asked. Recognising her Scottish accent, one of them said his grandfather was Jimmie—the Auld Alliance between Scots and French. I have already mentioned about our eventful visit to Amsterdam in its two hundredth year.

Mother had spent her honeymoon in Jersey, and so we went to Guernsey, hired a car, explored the island, and visited Herm. Much later, we returned to Jersey with her wheelchair for a BAPS meeting.

While I was working in London, on the spur of the moment we decided to go to Gibraltar and stayed in the Rock Hotel. Apart from Mother sitting on and breaking her spectacles, we did a day trip to Tangier under the guidance of a local in a fez. He got very annoyed when, on my own and despite language difficulties, I found a slipper maker and managed to buy a pair for each of us. He did not get his cut! I wanted a kaftan, which were all the rage then, to fit me despite being tall. He took us to a friend of his who quickly became exasperated because none of them fitted. He asked Mother if I was her daughter and then offered her twenty camels for me. Despite there being a meat shortage back in the UK, transport would be a problem, and so she declined. Our return to Gibraltar was via the airport.

Mother remarked that it was full of trench-coated men looking as if they were selling dirty postcards.

In London we had recently had a naval trainee doctor who was working now in Gibraltar. I had arranged to meet him for after-dinner drinks, but he was late. He apologetically explained that a newborn baby had just been delivered with a duodenal atresia (blockage on the way out of the stomach), and he asked if I could help. I insisted that he did the operation with my assistance. All the other doctors and nurses asked for my help. By way of thank-you, we were invited to HMS *Rook* (the shore headquarters) for drinks and then lunch with the senior surgeon, an ENT surgeon who had been born not far from Mother's birthplace. However, much more enjoyable was an evening with the juniors at a local Spanish restaurant. One of the other customers wondered whether Mummy was mother to all of us—difficult because one was Chinese, and the trainee I knew was Indian! Afterwards, we played skittles, but Mother forgot to let go of the ball and so had to run with it.

We returned to Norway with the Northern group of the MWIF. (an international group of medical women) Before the meeting in Oslo on their National day, we toured around, visiting a glacier and buying handmade shoes (which I still have) and jumpers. Unfortunately, the only vegetable we ever got were Brussels sprouts, and I did not like them even before the holiday.

Sometimes the holidays were Scottish based. Apart from Cullen (where my maternal grandmother was born), we visited the west coast. Mother was friendly with the wife of the factor of Cullen House, and so we also got to see round Cullen House before it was sold for flats. We stayed in the

Enilorac

hotel in Crinan at the beginning of the canal—a beautiful outlook and superb seafood. The owner's wife was an artist, and I still have yet to buy one of her paintings. Later, we discovered the Isle of Eriska Hotel (with badgers coming to the bar door at night), run by the former minister of St Andrews University. They had superb food, and even after Mummy became more disabled, they looked after us so well. We could tour up and down the west coast from our base in Benderloch, or we could wander round the island.

Despite its name, the British Association of Paediatric Surgeons is international, and so every three years its meeting is held overseas. The first such meeting for me was in Genoa in 1971. I revisited Oslo in 1977, making it part of a Scandinavian trip. Outside Oslo, I visited with parents of a university friend, Asfrid. Her father was interested in Old Norse, and we found a similarity between that and Scottish dialect words. This is not surprising because the Vikings were raping and pillaging the coasts of Scotland centuries ago. One of my close friends, Toby, was a Norwegian from Trondheim and always maintains we are related : because I was tall, blonde, and blue-eyed, one of his ancestors must have raped one of mine! After visiting paediatric surgical friends in Copenhagen, I went on to Gotenberg. Then I went to Stockholm and to the university town of Upsalla. Finland finished the tour, and visiting Tampere, Helsinki, and Turku. I learnt about saunas and Karelia and Finnish legends. In Turku we went out in a boat on the Baltic Sea, and it was beautiful, but oh, the mosquitoes! I was bitten alive even through trousers.

Another BAPS destination was Marseilles in 1979. My main recollection of this visit was eating bouillabaisse at the seafront and two taxis racing to get us back to our accommodation. Mother came with me to the meetings in Vienna in 1985 and Jersey in 1996, even though she was in a wheelchair by then. Other BAPS meetings were in Estoril in 2003, which I combined with a visit to Lisbon (an interesting and vibrant city, even on my own), and Dublin in 2005, which was my last meeting.

First with a British Council course and then with BAPS in 1997, I visited Istanbul. I got to know this amazing city, with the locals showing me all the sights and shopping in the Grand Bazaar. You discuss the traffic rather than the weather (as in UK).

I have visited Hungary several times, even before the Iron Curtain was knocked down. The first time was when my plane was late, and I missed the train from Budapest to Pecs. The only way to get to Pecs late at night was by a Budapest taxi. Because of my "interesting" journey to Pecs, Andrew decided that he would take me to Budapest by car at the end of the meeting. He also took a Japanese surgeon who was flying out that morning from Budapest. The host, Andrew, was very tired after having organised the meeting as well as hosting an evening with his colleague and their wives, me, the Japanese surgeon, and a Finn. By the end of the evening, the Finn was saying syranawa(goodbye) to the one of the Hungarian wives. The journey north to Budapest consisted of me yelling Andrew's name to try to keep him awake. Over breakfast at the airport, the Japanese man revealed that his flight was at ten o'clock, not nine as he had led us to believe. Andrew visibly shrank, and we quickly retired to find a friend from Trier in central Budapest, who was to show me Budapest and accompany me to Vienna. We poured black coffee into Andrew and sent him on his way; thankfully, he got home safely.

On another occasion on the way to Szeged, Hungary, with Mother, she made friends with the local mayor, who was making a huge cauldron of goulash. He gave her some paprika and got her to taste the goulash. In Szeged she lost her wedding ring. We were staying in a student residence, and she had taken it off to put on an eternity ring I had given her. On return to the UK, she still had no ring but said that it would turn up. It had been given in love and was pure gold, so it would come back to her. I was very doubtful. My Hungarian friend Andrew wrote to tell me that a ring had been found by the cleaner, who had handed it to the organisers of the meeting. According to the description of the engraving, it was Mother's. He could not send it because it would have been stolen by the officials (in contrast to the honesty of the cleaner). It would be returned to us when someone was allowed to leave Hungary for a meeting. This occurred some months later, when Andrew himself went to India via Moscow and Afghanistan. In India, he met with one of my colleagues for another meeting and entrusted the ring to him. After six months, I was no longer a bastard. At the next meeting in Hungary, Mother was surrounded by doctors wanting to kiss the ring.

My first visit to Vienna was on my own. Later, Mother and I visited that elegant city, staying in the Sacher Hotel just off the Ringstrasse. On that occasion, on our way home at the airport, we heard, "Carolina, Carolina!" This was a Polish surgeon returning from a meeting in Graz. Mother looked heavenwards and said, "Not again." Once, we were going to Copenhagen from Manchester. Our plane was late, and as we stood in the passport queue, someone in the other queue said, "Hullo." This was Narin, who had been in the year below me at university. Once we got through passport control, I was surprised to see him talking with Ole, our Danish host. Narin, then president of College of Obstetricians in London, was enquiring about boats to Malmo, and Ole asked about the Manchester plane; they got talking. It really is a small world. Vienna is a beautiful city, but I prefer Budapest because she is equally beautiful but shows signs of her past, which makes her have more character.

I first met Ivan, a Hungarian doctor from Pecs, in Munich when he had recently escaped to the West with his girlfriend. Gesine, my Austrian friend, was in charge of him but wished to have dinner with someone else. Ivan joined Andrew, whom he knew; my Finnish friend, Eero; and me. Despite his poor English, we had a super dinner. It emerged that he had no place to sleep, and Eero offered him the spare bed in his room. Andrew left us, and we went to inspect the room. We had drunk a quantity of wine and beer, and the two of them decided to walk me back to the hotel, stopping for "another little drink" on the way as we wove our way toward the hotel. At a meeting in Graz, I met Ivan again, who had been with us in Munich. Ivan's English improved over the years I knew him—enough to tell me rude stories while driving Mother and me to functions in Hungary. He knew Mother was deaf and so kept checking to make sure she was not hearing him. I was sure she was!

Early on in my career in Manchester, I won a scholarship from the *British Journal of Surgery* to travel in the United States, going to Atlanta, Houston, Los Angeles, and Kansas City. In each place I stayed with surgical colleagues who showed me round their cities and departments. In Atlanta, it was all about the Battle of Atlanta (from the Civil War). In Houston, I remember trying to teach my Hungarian friend how to play backgammon—in a swimming pool. In Los Angeles, I learnt the delights of a Jacuzzi under the clear Californian skies, drinking local white wine. My host offered me his car to drive along Hollywood Boulevard, but I declined. I watched one surgeon performing a small operation on an infant that took the time for the Space Shuttle to land (which was happening then). Usually I would take fifteen to twenty minutes. Fortunately, in another hospital I assisted another surgeon who worked more in line with British standards of time.

The only place I knew no one was Denver. However, one of the surgeons there was an expert in biliary atresia. He was initially unwilling to have me visit (perhaps because I was a woman?), but by the end of my visit, he wanted me to stay longer. He introduced me to Rocky Mountain Oysters (sheep's testicles) and had me operate—a change of opinion. Easter was spent in Kansas City with one of the ex-GOS thoracic trainees, Keith, which was delightful. Next was the wilds of Indiana to stay with a old school friend, Evelyn, one of my golf mates who was involved in the gin fiasco when we were schoolgirls before university. She was a redhead and had married a Rhodes Scholar (also a redhead) whom she'd met at St Andrews University. They had six red-headed children and lived in the back woods—a marked contrast to the opulence elsewhere. This was the only non-working time for me. I found the scholarship very useful by introducing me to new ideas, and more especially new people with whom I would keep in contact.

I continued by attending the retirement party (lasting three days) in Philadelphia for a surgeon who was about to become the Surgeon General of the United States. In the past, he had made me earrings, a hobby of his. However, no one should have a retirement party for three days! At the final dinner in a gentlemen's club, the evening was a dance-and-eat affair. A very small, bald Japanese surgeon (who had invented the operation for biliary atresia) asked me to dance. He fitted under my right bosom with a beatific smile on his face. I could not laugh because the movement of my bosom would have touched his bald head. I came off the floor saying, "I don't know why he asked me …!"

Our table was near the door and consisted of me, Joe Cohen (my colleague), an American surgeon from the West Coast, a local neurosurgeon, a surgeon who thought he was God's gift to women, and a very old local couple (he having been a paediatrician). We were suddenly joined by a woman in a tight-fitting dress who sat next to the old man and proceeded to stroke his neck! God's Gift asked her to dance in the hope of breaking this up. She looked him up and down and said, "Why should I?" but still went with him. By the time they returned to the table, he stated that she was either on drugs or drunk. He placed her well away from the old couple, and she now sat on the West Coast surgeon's knee, steaming up his spectacles. I had decided that she was a prostitute looking for a lift home, despite the others' disbelief. I was proved right by one of the club officers.

A meeting of BAPS held in Chios was interesting—not so much for the papers as for the trips elsewhere. We went by hovercraft to Kushadasi in Turkey, to visit Ephesus. Mother and I found these Roman remains very interesting.

Because of our mutual liking for Turkish coffee, we wanted to buy the special coffee pots. Our guide would not let us buy those being sold by souvenir vendors because they had been specially treated; he would find some proper ones for us. While waiting for our boat back to Chios, he took the group to a carpet shop. We were given mint tea and shown beautiful carpets. Mother fell for a silk one that had the tree of life pattern. Of course they could send it to me—and they took credit cards! My reaction was, "I love you dearly, Mother, but it is too expensive."

By this time, the owner said to Mother, "Your daughter?" She answered yes and was offered ten camels for me (down from the offer in Tangier).

Mother replied, "Not enough," and seemed prepared to bargain—to my horror. We were saved by the guide appearing and saying, "Coffee pots." To the disgust of the shopkeeper, we left and got our proper coffee pots. I asked her about the interplay, and she said that she wanted to see how far he would go! Samir, our Lebanese friend, said, "Honest to God, Mrs Doig, a good racing camel is worth a thousand pounds." So much for friendship!

My next visit to Greece was on my own, to Athens in 1988. I had visited previously with Mother. I went earlier than the meeting because of a cheaper flight and managed to see a paediatrician who had worked with me in Durham. Connie and I had watched the film *Never on a Sunday* together, and he had told me what was actually being said. I managed to meet up with Gesine from Austria, who was also early, and we had an enjoyable weekend relaxing. We had cemented our friendship looking for female loos in Santa Marguita years before. Also at the official meeting was another Greek, Stavros, who had been in GOS with me. A couple I knew who were working in Saudi Arabia were there without luggage, the airline having lost it. Mother had remarked I had too many clothes, but it was useful to be able to lend Hanna some—and to comment to Mother on my return that they had all been worn! James, her husband, said that it was very strange to look at us and know the clothes were all mine.

After retirement, in 2000 I went to the BAPS meeting in Sorrento. I went to very little of the meeting, instead going on the women's programme, which included visits to Pompeii and Herculaneum. I am very interested in all things Roman, and this appealed to me. We even got to climb to the top of Vesuvius, which was very dusty and stained our shoes. At the beginning of the meeting, I ran into Michael, Samir's(one of my former trainees in Manchester) boss in Beirut. Michael had arrived with no luggage. He hired a car and took me shopping, and then we had a delightful lunch down by the beach at Positano, along the Amalfi coast. I think I preferred that to my later holiday in Rome, despite being entertained there by a fellow paediatric surgeon, Carlo. He showed Helen (a medical friend of mine) and me round the city and took us out of Rome to Hadrian's Palace.

The Christmas of the year Mother died (1997), Samir insisted I come to Lebanon and not be alone. We visited all the important places of interest, such as Bylbos, the oldest inhabited city, and Baalbeck (now sadly damaged). We went south to Sidon, where Madeleine, his wife, and I went on Boxing Day. The guide was delighted to show us round this Crusader castle, with Madeleine translating his Arabic. As we left to buy some delectable sweet meats, a bus full of

Enilorac

Japanese tourists arrived. I remarked that Lebanon would be all right now. This was very soon after the war. Christmas was spent at the Cedars of Lebanon, where Madeleine's parents had a farm. She had two sisters, and because all three had numerous children, there was no chance of me being lonely. The conversation was in a mixture of English, French, and Arabic—and sometimes all three in one sentence. Samir could show me the green line, which had split Beirut and the dreadful damage at the museum.

On this visit, he insisted that I not work, but the next time I was to lecture. This happened two years later. I had been examining for the Edinburgh College in Hong Kong and was very tired on my arrival in Beirut. Samir wanted to take me to a new restaurant, the first of its kind in Lebanon. I told him either I went to dinner and did not lecture the next day, or he let me go to sleep so that I could function at the meeting. He agreed to the latter, saying, "But it's the first Chinese restaurant in Lebanon." After a fortnight of being entertained in Hong Kong, that was the last thing I needed! While in Hong Kong, I had read in the *South China Times* that the best way to make money in the world then was to be a Lebanese builder, and it was true. We walked along the Corniche, and all the ruins were gone. Opposite the museum, the block of flats that had been in ruins with trees growing out of it was now rebuilt and occupied.

The college, once one was established as an examiner, required you to examine overseas. Kuwait, my first time as an examiner overseas, was just before the war with Iraq. Initially I had visited my former trainees from Manchester, Samir (from Lebanon), and Rang (a Kurd from Iraq) in Al Ain. They used me as a role model for the women students, and I had to give talks. Rang's mother was visiting, and she taught me how to barter on a shopping trip to Dubai. This made me popular with the wives when we went shopping in Kuwait. Although it was thought it would be too difficult for me to examine in Saudi Arabia, I had no problems in Kuwait, apart from an Egyptian who thought he knew more anatomy than me—and he did not!

Singapore and Hong Kong followed on numerous occasions, allowing me to know both cities and the surgeons. Unfortunately, we were kept busy, but we did manage some time to sightsee and shop—one of my sins. At meetings I would sometimes become a lady and attend the accompanying person's programme, which was usually more interesting. Mother visited both cities on more than one occasion, both when able-bodied and when in a wheelchair. Like me, she liked all things Chinese. When she was younger, a paternal uncle had wanted her to come out to Singapore to teach, and so she was interested to see where she might have been. She also came with me to Kuala Lumpur, and afterwards we holidayed in Penang. While in Kuala Lumpur, on a free day we went to a temple with a very long flight of steps. We were caught in a monsoon rainstorm, and one lady's dress became transparent, showing her polka dot underpants. We rallied round in the back of the bus to eventually make her respectable. The day after we arrived in KL to examine, I was required to examine. I am afraid I was on automatic pilot because I was so tired. In Penang, one of my former trainees took us both to the hawker market where we chose dishes from different stalla and then sat at tables to eat.

On one such visit to Hong Kong, I was taken by Chinese friends to see snakes, the gall bladders of which were extracted

Enilorac

without killing them. The bile was apparently helpful to men! As well as entertainment every night by different people, we always went to the races, either at Happy Valley on Hong Kong Island or at Shatin in the New Territories. Although I had been taken to the Grand National by one of my Manchester surgical colleagues, I knew very little about horse racing and betting. I was soon educated by one of the guests at the lunch. Much hilarity was voiced because a recent British government report had just come out stating, "Since betting was alien to the Chinese character....." Nothing could have been further from the truth.

On Mother's last visit to Hong Kong, we were taken to lunch by a delightful Chinese orthopaedic surgeon, who was also a member of the Jockey Club. The dining room had been used when the Queen visited. Harry wanted to take Mother to the Great Wall of China, and he reluctantly agreed I could go too. Even in a wheelchair, Mother did not miss out, being lifted from boat to boat by the college officer when we went for dinner in a fishing village. The next day, she remarked that it had been a long time since she was bruised (on her arms) by a man. Apart from the formal meals arranged for us, I managed to have lunch with a Chinese general surgeon friend in a fishing village along Hong Kong's mainland coast; we chose our fish swimming in the tank. I did manage to do some shopping too. I also had dinner with a paediatric surgeon who is now head of that department in Hong Kong. On one visit, the college helped to found the Hong Kong College of Surgeons, a magnificent affair.

Because two former trainees of mine were in Singapore—Carolyn (by now head of department) and Ram (my Indian friend from Booth Hall)—I spent the coming millennium in Singapore: Christmas with a Chinese flavour and New Year with an Indian flavour. I sent a fax to Johanna, a friend in England, dated 2000—which she received in 1999. Radica, Ram's wife, arranged for me to have a sari. I also went silk shopping and had clothes made by Miss Ming, and later I got a Chinese cheosam outfit made. I discovered I was a tiger and was born in the tiger hour—a combination that makes me dangerous according to the Chinese horoscope.

My first overseas meeting with Edinburgh College was to Deauville in the north of France. I had been attending a meeting at St Mark's Hospital in London about colonic problems, and I had to arrive late, flying into the very small airport in a five-seater plane from London. This meeting was combined with the French and Egyptian surgeons. I managed to laze by the pool at the hotel, and a small child was playing with his negro nanny when his father appeared. He recognised me and said hello, causing consternation amongst my friends. He had been one of our trainees from South Africa in GOS, in London.

I visited Australia with the Edinburgh College for a combined meeting in Adelaide, with its broad streets. After the meeting, which was excellent, I decided to see some of Australia and so visited Sydney and Queensland. In Cairns, I even managed to scuba dive on the Great Barrier Reef despite being an old lady. It was beautiful, but it was just as well I had an instructor because I kept wanting to take the breathing tube out of my mouth—not a good idea! I finished the Australian leg at Uluru. Seeing it early in the morning with the changing colours was mind-blowing.

An anaesthetist friend from GOS days, Malcolm, insisted I visit him and his wife in Dunedin, New Zealand.

We toured round, going to the albatrosses at their sanctuary and then to Queenstown. We even experienced a New Zealand traffic jam: a flock of sheep! He took me to a winery at Bannockburn. New Zealand is like Britain years ago; I could have lived there. I visited New Zealand a second time, seeing some of North Island. Upon arriving in Auckland, I went north to the Bay of Islands and right to the tip of the island before coming south in a bus on Nine Mile Beach. Being driven on sand was an interesting experience. Rotorua followed, with bathing in the hot springs. I was fortunate enough to have a charming Maori taxi driver to show me around the area and explain matters to me. I then had to visit Dunedin again—a city named after Edinburgh—to visit Malcolm and Gaye.

Edinburgh College had overseas meetings in Kenya, India, Pakistan, Kuala Lumpur, and Hong Kong, where I gave talks as well as listened to lectures. In 1987, I was very keen to visit Kenya and the rest of Africa, as Father had been there during the war. He had played golf on the Nairobi golf course. I was taken up to a vantage point overlooking the Rift Valley, and it was awesome. After the meeting, I met up with my ex trainees in Kenya. A group of surgeons (and wives) went on safari, going to Ambeseli, Tsavo, and finishing in Mombasa (another place associated with Daddy). I adore elephants and enjoyed it immensely. I can remember waking up in the morning in my mud hut, drinking my morning tea, and looking at snow-capped Kilimanjaro. We finished the safari with a champagne birthday party for one of the people in the people carrier. I would have liked to see more of Africa, but Mummy was unhappy about me being there. It was some time later that she said that Africa had taken my father from her, and she was frightened it would do the same with me.

Another Edinburgh College meeting was held in India in 1990, starting in Bombay (now Mumbai), where I was looked after by Sam and his wife. He had been working with me in GOS and was now an urologist. Seeing India with them was eye-opening and gave me a true feeling of the place. Madras (Chennai) followed, where we danced on the beach, and two of us went round a swimming pool in a rickshaw! Much more formal was New Delhi, with its crowds and traffic. I wore a dress that I had made for me in Bombay; sadly, it no longer fits. I met Sam at a meeting in Singapore, much to the surprise of the receptionist many years later.

After the meeting, a group of us went to Rajahstan, Agra, and the Taj Mahal. The rain was so heavy that the Edinburgh council ended up in bare feet with trousers rolled up. In Jaipur, apart from jewellery shopping, we went up to the Amber Fort by elephant, much to my delight. We also attended an elephant polo match, where the elephants kept standing on the ball. This was during Holi, a Hindu religious holiday, and so we and everyone else were rainbow coloured because multi-coloured dust was flung around. Before we left for our final destination, Udiapur, my jeweller gave me a beautifully carved elephant. We stayed in Udiapur in the Lake Palace Hotel. Unfortunately, the marble round the swimming pool was slippery, and I fell and sustained a scaphoid fracture at my wrist, which was not diagnosed until I got home. We visited many of the sights, including the elephant stables at Fatepur Sikri (thankfully no longer in use).

Enilorac

The English College also had overseas meetings. During the president's time in office, the meeting had two separate destinations. As I have already mentioned, I visited Barbados with them when they gave an honorary fellowship to the governor of St Kitts. Bert was a big man, and I had known him when he was training in obstetrics in Dundee. Everyone was surprised when he greeted me with a big hug. We then travelled to the States, visiting New York, Harvard, and Yale. In New York, we stayed just off Central Park, and I managed to go to the theatre near Times Square with a colleague. I did not care for Boston because we appeared to be a nuisance. Very few of the local doctors attended the meeting, and they did not bother to tell others of our visit to the Medical Society (many would have entertained us had they known). Yale was much better, and I liked New Haven and the people there.

I returned to Africa after Mother's death in late 1997, revisiting Kenya and my ex trainees on my way to Durban and Cape Town with the English College. The college meeting was at Victoria Falls, which was awesome and very wet. We flew over the falls in a helicopter—after being individually weighed! On that occasion, before the meeting I went on safari in Botswana, staying in a tented camp. Breakfast was round the campfire, and we travelled in Jeeps and boats on the river to see animals and birds. I visited a university friend in Johannesburg and met up with Fred, who had been my co-registrar in Durham. He took me to the hospital in Soweto, where he worked.

A Irish friend of mine who was on the English College council thought it would be a good idea for me to go to the Irish College meeting in Durban that year. Although

I only knew Brendan; his wife, Ann; and some paediatric surgeons, I decided to go because Daddy was buried there, at Stellawood cemetery. Brendan's wife came with me to the cemetery overlooking the bay, and I left some of Mummy's ashes on his grave. I was very grateful to Ann for being there.

I knew very few people, the content of the meeting was general surgery, and I had a broken wrist, so I attended the ladies programme. One of the ladies, who was very officious, asked me who my husband was. After a pause, I remarked, "I don't have one." After another pause, I added, "At least, not one of my own!" I could not help myself, and she turned away, horrified. The other ladies were delighted because she had been a nuisance to them all.

In Cape Town, we were based near the waterfront and enjoyed excellent food in the evenings. Apart from going up Table Mountain, going out to Robyn Island, and taking the train to Stellenbosch (the wine area), I managed to meet up with the local paediatric surgeons in the Red Cross hospital. I needed to buy a bigger suitcase at the end of this holiday. After my retirement, I went with English College to Singapore and Hong Kong on separate occasions. They were rather surprised at how many general surgeons and orthopaedic surgeons I knew.

The visit to Singapore in 2004 also included going to Darwin, Australia. Apart from visiting Kakadoo, a beautiful and wild place, I went shopping for pearls. These were known as *the* pearls because they were expensive, and it took me long time to pay them off. Unlike the other women on the trip, I did not needed to ask my husband about them—I bought them there and then. Upon my return to the hotel, all the ladies came to my room to try them on.

Enilorac

The visit to China in 2007 was not without incident. I do seem to be accident prone. We began in Hong Kong, where I went shopping because I knew it well. At a reception at the Peak, I fell down a black marble step and cracked a rib, limiting me somewhat. We visited the tea-growing area around Guilin in the south and sailed up the Li River, the mountains on either side looking just like Chinese paintings. I bought some jade, of course. Although we were based in Beijing, we visited Shi'an and the terracotta Warriors, which were unbelievable. I was not able to walk much of the Great Wall because of my rib being painful. I required a stick, but this gave me time to look at the stalls, and I bought some Chinese paintbrushes. We finished up in Shanghai, a cosmopolitan city with many high-rise buildings.

With a female fellow named Helen (who's now sadly dead), I went to a MWF meeting in Iceland. It was a strange but beautiful country with huge waterfalls and black volcanic sand. We swam (or rather, lazed) in the Blue Lagoon, a hot spa that was invigorating. With Helen and two friends from GOS days, I went up the coast of Norway in the Hurtigruten ship. I enjoyed this because as well as being a cruise, the ship delivered goods and people to all the towns on the way north. Trondheim was first port of call after starting in Bergen, where we were met and looked after by Toby, the local paediatric surgeon who thinks we are related. Alesund, an art deco town, was the site of a monument to the Shetland bus (boats which plied across the North Sea during World War II). We visited Tromso and the Arctic Cathedral, as well as the North Cape. We met with Suomi people and their reindeer. We even stopped at a place called Ultima Thule- the end of the world. I think there a few of them around the world. We went as far north as Kirkenes, next to the Russian border, before coming back down the coast to Bergen, where we had started. During our return south, three of us had a Jacuzzi on the deck within the Arctic Circle. We spent a few days afterwards in Bergen, visiting amongst other things Grieg's house at Trollhagen.

With the surgical section of the Royal Society of Medicine (RSM), I travelled to Jordan, visiting Amman, Petra, and Acaba. Again I had hurt my ankle and so was not able to walk far. On a visit north of Amman, I got left behind at a major Roman site. I was unable to walk and retreated back to the Arabic shops at the entrance. Unfortunately, our guide forgot about me, and I required the tourist police to ring round to find which restaurant could accommodate the number in our group. Afterwards, the bus driver always made sure that I was on board. We visited the Dead Sea, and floating on the sea was remarkable. Wadi Rum was interesting, but best of all was Petra. Although I could not go to the High Place, I went down towards the treasury on a donkey. Acaba was relaxing after our various sightseeing.

I continue to travel since retirement, usually in the company of my friend Winifred. Most recently we went to the Antarctic via Buenos Aires, which was something I always wanted to do. This was on the same ship and with the same captain as we had had on our trip to the Cape Verde islands. (More later) I have now visited all seven continents. Despite travelling extensively, I have yet to visit Japan or any of the Pacific islands.

12

Friendship

Of all the means which wisdom acquires to ensure happiness through out the whole of life, by far the most important is friendship.
—Epicurus *Lives of Eminent Philosophers*

At junior school, I made friends with Vivian. We were both blonde, blue-eyed babies in the park with our mothers. They had a television, and so Mummy and I watched the coronation with them. The only problem was she lived at the other end of town. I would visit their caravan in Arbroath when staying with my grandparents for the holidays. Although the friendship lasted throughout our school days, when I moved away from Forfar, we lost track of each other. After our class reunion in Perth in 2010, we reconnected as before. She still lives in Forfar, and she is married with three grown-up children. Another school friend has moved with her husband to Spain. As a child, I would play with two sisters, Nancy and Alice, whose father also had a drapers shop.

At senior school, four of us would regularly play golf and spend Saturday nights going to the pictures. Evelyn, went to St Andrews University and met her husband-to-be, a Rhodes Scholar from America. I last saw her when I visited the States. Isobel is also on the other side of the pond in Canada. Her mother was a teacher, and during the summer vacation, we would cook for our mothers, phoning each other to check what we were giving them. It was an excellent way to learn to cook and to experiment. She has managed to come with her husband to one of the reunions.

Helen lived nearby and went to Aberdeen University like Isobel, reading geography. She became a curator in the Hunterian Museum in Glasgow. Unfortunately, she has since died of cancer. Also part of this group (but non-golf players) were Ruth and Helena. Ruth was very short but had a bright personality. She now lives in Edinburgh, and so I can see her when she is in town. Her husband is a workaholic and travels much. The one I have lost touch with is Helena. With a Polish father and Turkish mother, she spoke several languages and did English at university. It was her lawn I fell off, when I broke my ankle as a teenager,. She introduced me to Turkish coffee, which became a favourite of mine.

Lewis I have already mentioned from school days and before. He lived nearby, and we would play various sports together. It was after meeting Ruth and Lewis in Edinburgh that we started the school class reunions.

At university, again I was part of a group. Jane was my closest friend, whom I had met at the bursary competition. She is a Yorkshire lass who became an anaesthetist but, because of a neurological disease, had to give it up to become a general practitioner. She is married with two daughters.

Enilorac

Although we may not speak for some time, when we do it is as if we had met yesterday. We know each other very well.

The rest of the group consisted of Meg, who now lives near London; I have met her in town, but not often enough. There was also Edna, a Dundonian who became an obstetrician in Birmingham; like me, she never married. It was unfortunate that she appeared to be jealous when I got my consultant post before she got hers. Sadly, she has since died.

Many of my friends are shorter than me, which is not too difficult. In Glasgow Sick Kids hospital, I met Ann from London. She had studied at St Mary's in Paddington and so knew my tall friend David (of magic circle fame). We first met when we were both unsuccessful for a junior houseman's post in Great Ormond Street Hospital, and then we remet in Glasgow. I would see her when I was in London for examinations and interviews, and she and her husband would give me dinner before putting me on the night sleeper train north. It was fortunate that she ended up working in anaesthetics in GOS when I was there. We continue to be close to this day, and I consider her my second oldest friend.

At GOS I became friendly with a pathology senior registrar, Jean. She was a member of the Medical Women's Federation and became a consultant in paediatric pathology in Edinburgh—two reasons why she reappeared in my life once I had retired. It is strange how many people keep coming back into my life; friends do seem to be for life.

My time in Manchester meant I worked closely with my secretary, Irene. We developed an excellent working relationship and forged a deep friendship which continues. I am phoned every so often to check that I am okay. I am godmother to her son Ben. I developed relationships with colleagues' wives, especially Liz, whose urologist husband I first met at the English College examinations. She helped me when Mother died, and I still see her when I am in Manchester. When I decided to come back to Scotland, she spoke to Irene to try to dissuade me from leaving Manchester and living in the "back of beyond". When she and her husband, Ray, visited me in Heriot, she had the good grace to say she had been wrong.

I made friends with many of my trainees, both male and female. Perina, Navid, and Ram have already been mentioned. I am friendly with Ram's wife, Radica. While visiting them in Singapore she arranged for me to buy a sari, all without telling Ram until I did my fashion show. She likes to shop, and so we can get up to mischief together. Once I retired, we would meet at least once a year; either Radica and her family visit me in Scotland, or I visit them in Leeds. A retirement complex was built next door to their house, but she could not see inside because she was not over seventy. We went together on the pretext that I might wish to stay near them. It meant we were given a complete showing, but then I said I had to think about it! Ram was horrified at our audacity.

One of my trainees from Singapore, Carolyn, is another who phones to check up on me. She has since moved from Singapore to be near her parents in Perth, Australia. Mother called her Little Caroline, and I was Big Caroline. We developed a close friendship, and I visited her for the millennium in Singapore. In Singapore one gentleman made us both blush. I liked to say that I am like good wine (ageing well). He remarked that you lay good wine on its back! Carolyn says she is like a banana since she is chinese and yellow on the outside but white inside. His reply was that you peeled a banana! Once I returned to Scotland and settled close to Edinburgh, I had another companion for shopping, although she was worse than I am! Audrey was the wife of one of the surgeons connected to the Edinburgh College, and she recently died.

Within two years of my retirement in 2000, I had made another close friend: Winifred. We were both Soroptimists in Edinburgh, but I had difficulty attending meetings. At a friendship meeting, they were speaking about golf, and she turned to me and said, "You don't play golf." I replied I did but had not played since coming north. I had been a member of a golf club in Manchester but had only managed to play about once a year (with a fellow Scottish doctor). Although I became a member of a golf club in Dalkeith, I had not played there because of various injuries: falling down Castle Hill in Budapest on a wet leaf and breaking my ankle (again), and falling off a jet ski in Barbados and pulling my shoulder muscles.

She immediately organised for us to play together the following Tuesday. We started to play golf regularly although she is much better than I am. She's non-medical and a widow, and she is an excellent teacher and has improved my golf a little. She has a wry sense of humour. Once when I bemoaned the fact that there was no seat at a distant tee, she remarked that she would bequeath one when I died. She is five years older than I am! We still play golf together, now at Kilspindie golf course at Aberlady, down the coast from Edinburgh. But now I need a golf buggie between holes because of my back. People tend to think we have known each other for many years, but in fact it is only seventeen years.

She has a unique way of dealing with pavement rage—a common problem in Edinburgh during the festival. The Dalai Lama suggests that when people annoy you, they have been put there to test you. Under your breath, you say, "Dalai Lama," and your anger immediately disappears. It works!

We found that although we have different tastes and varying views, we get on well together. We went on courses together, cooking, art and go bird watching with the Scottish Ornithological Club. Those various activities lead to us holidaying together. Even if we have to share a room or cabin we can survive without rancour. We have travelled (usually by boat) around Europe and farther afield, not without incident. Despite being older, she is always ready for adventure and mischief, and she makes me feel ancient sometimes.

Our first foray together was on the Danube at New Year, sailing from Budapest, which we both knew well, to Vienna, where we were for Hogmanay. We heard the church bells from the top deck of the river boat. We visited Bratislava (in the mist), Melk, and Salzburg. This was a successful trip, and so we decide to travel together again. We travelled up and down the Douro River from Oporto. While having a black currant ice cream at the Mateus Rose estate, the portable seat I was sitting on collapsed, and I slowly descended to the ground—with no stain on my white slacks. We were taken for a rustic meal near where we berthed at the end of the river in Portugal. Winifred bit into a piece of pork and broke her tooth, requiring a visit to a Portuguese-speaking dentist.

We were taken by bus from there to Salamaca in Spain, an old university town full of tourists and gypsies. We were told to watch our bags and to not put anything in back pockets. Of course, someone did, and his wallet was stolen. Lunch was in a large hotel with for entertainment flamenco dancers. The ladies' powder room and cubicles was remarkable—mirrors all round on ceiling, floor and walls—gosh! On returning to our table, one of our party inadvertently cut her leg on an upturned chair, necessitating my services to deal with it. The wound healed well, even if she was the wrong age group for me to treat. On the way back down the river at the Sandeman Estate, I sat in a nest of ants! By the time we reached Oporto again, we were missing one passenger—he had suffered a retinal detachment in one of his eyes. What a journey!

Our visit to Madeira was great, even if the airport was closed the day after we arrived because of bad weather and the island had the first snow in living memory. One bus trip, we could see nothing because of the mist but we did journey down a steep hill by basket.

Undeterred, we decided next to go to Libya. I am interested in Roman ruins and wished to visit Lepto Magna. This coincided with the Libyan war, so no go. We were both desperate for a holiday and accepted the alternative programme arranged by the travel company: a mystery North Mediterranean cruise. We had a few days in Malta before setting sail for Sicily, Sardinia, and the Egadi Islands. This satisfied my wish for Roman artefacts. The Egadi Islands were small fishing villages unaccustomed to cruise ships, however small. Thence, we visited Minorca, where I shopped for jewellery and bought a pair of sandals at a nunnery.

Formentero followed, with a bus taking us to the top of the island after a coffee stop with fig cake. Winifred persuaded two girls to lend us their Vespa, but we did not drive it but we were photographed. We did get to visit North Africa, sailing into Melilla, a Spanish enclave, on a Sunday morning. They had had no tourists for more than six months and so greeted us with enthusiasm, but we did have to leave before lunch because the boat from Spain was due then and needed the berth. This whole trip was finished off by sailing through the Straits of Gibraltar and up the river to Seville, an interesting city that I would like to visit for longer. It helped that Winifred speaks Spanish. All this was for a reduced cost because we had stayed with the company.

Sailing on the waterways of Russia between Moscow and St Petersburg was next. I liked St Petersburg (Winifred wants to visit in the snow) but did not care for Moscow. I found the travel on the various waterways boring because apart from numerous locks, the scenery was always the same: riverbank and trees, with no hills in the background.

In contrast we decided to go to the Cape Verde Islands. Each island is completely different. One, Fogo, had had a volcanic eruption less than six months before we arrived, but because no one had died, it had not featured in the world media. It was interesting to visit and still see the smoke and lava. The winery that was damaged still managed to provide us with some wine to taste. All facilities had been damaged, and so there were no toilets. It was a case of ladies to the left behind the trees and bushes, and gentlemen to the right in the lava field. When we reached the main tourist island, Sal, the local pilot, came in to dock too quickly and hit the quay. Winifred was up top and saw it happen. I was still in our cabin and hit the wardrobe door when the ship stopped. I split my head open and bled profusely because I was on Warfarin. The ship's doctor, Chris, had to stitch me up—fourteen stitches of different types, and without any local anaesthetic. It was fortunate that I could trust him because he had been on two separate committees with me, in the Edinburgh Council and the GMC. Winifred learnt new skills of dab and cut the stitches. I had a secondary bleed; things always go wrong when you have a medical patient. It was necessary to bandage my head in a turban. Winifred brought me a feather duster when I said that I needed a feather or jewel to decorate it. In the end, I made a bandana to cover it and was called the bandana kid.

We then sailed across the sea to North Africa, visiting Marrakesh. The journey there by bus was interesting, not least because of the fertile land. We stopped in a field for a natural break to discover a lot of carpets, cushions, and low tables with a variety of drinks. A series of Portaloos had opposite them a stand with a mirror, a kettle with hot water, a basin, and a proper towel—all very civilised. When we stopped for a superb Moroccan lunch on the way to Marrekesh in another field, the Portaloos were each in individual tents, though the flaps did not always close properly.

A trip down the west coast of Scotland in May was to see birds because we are both keen bird watchers. Most of the birds (like puffins) had yet to arrive, and the weather was interesting. Our first stop in Stornaway followed snow the night before so that the grass at the Callanish stones was wet. Despite taking care, I fell again. I could not understand why I had such a large bruise over my right shoulder and bosom until I remembered I was on Warfarin (a blood thinner). We managed to land at St Kilda, walk along the main street, and stand in the school room. It was bleak, and the next stop, Iona, was a washout with driving rain. The weather in Anglesey was superb, and we did see some cloughs. However by the time we sailed to south Wales, the weather worsened. The ship had to shelter next to Stromer, which was being evacuated because of the strong winds. We were due to go to the Scilly Islands, but the captain decided that it would be better to aim for Falmouth before finishing in Plymouth. I now know what it is like to sail before a storm up the English Channel in a force eleven gale.

We went back to river cruising, going down the Rhine from Basel to Amsterdam. We visited, amongst other places, Strasbourg and Amsterdam again. Recently we returned to the waterways of Hungary, visiting many of the places where I had been many years before: Budapest, Pecs, and Szeged. How things have changed—for the better. We both like small ships with not too many passengers.

We also spend time together, apart from golf at Aberlady. This course is pleasant because we can view the wildlife (birds and seals) if we are not playing well. Winifred has a time share in Aviemore, and I sometimes go with her so that we can explore the area and perhaps see red squirrels.

Through Winifred, I met Ann, an Irish girl who was "a slave in red wellies". She helped as a gardener when I became unable to tend to my largish garden. She became a friend to both Winifred and me. Recently I have had to get another gardener because I am unable to do the work myself due to my back.

During my time at the GMC I got to know Johanna, who is from Folkestone and is non-medical. When I was chairman of the overseas committee, she came as what someone called "the new lay". That got us laughing, and we quickly became firm friends, contacting each other at least weekly. She is slightly older than me but does not behave as such. One of our adventures was with her gorgeous Mercedes Benz car. This had belonged to her husband (now dead), who had bought it new from the factory in 1956. I was staying with her in Folkestone when she left me in charge at an air show and laughed as I tried to deal with the questions from interested men. I accompanied her to various car rallies such as at Goodwood. One weekend we took the car ferry across to Bologne, which we could see from her house in Folkstone on a clear day. We had a great day eating and buying sexy red underwear.

When the London Eye was about to be opened, Johanna got a free pass to go on it because by then she had a flat opposite in Whitehall. Six ladies of a certain age took advantage of this, supposedly living in said flat. The fact that it was only one room made no difference. She had procured the flat when she was on the GMC because of being involved in a long and difficult case.

She phoned me to ask me to go on a Champagne rally in 1999. I do not like champagne, or rather I did not back then. We went across the Channel through the tunnel on the train, but the car would not come off. With difficulty we got going on our way to Rheims. We broke down on the motorway slowly coming to a stop on the hard shoulder. We were assisted by a garbage man who said he would get help, but we had no red triangle and so used my red jacket to warn of our breakdown. When the low loader arrived for the car, we went up in front to arrive in Rheims in a thunderstorm, with the klaxon on the breakdown lorry stuck making a dreadful noise. At the Mercedes Benz garage, everyone came out to look; the car is a looker. Johanna wanted no one to touch the car until we returned to the UK, so "Ne touchez pas". Now we were on a car rally without a car. Alain, the organiser of the event, came to our rescue: we could go with him.

The following morning, breakfast was at one of the champagne houses, consisting of coffee, croissants, and champagne. Our mid-morning stop was more champagne with lunch at a local vineyard, which served more champagne. It was the time of the vendange (grape harvest), and so there were lots of slow-moving tractors. Most of the cars were very old and could not go quickly—no time trials. One driver was delighted to get a speeding ticket in one village. Alain's Mustang broke down, and so two old ladies ended up pushing it up a hill.

That night was the formal dinner in yet another champagne house, with different champagnes for each course. I ended up between two French men who did not speak English, and my French is very poor. Johanna had the very dishy chief of police next to her. At lunch the next day at, we stopped at—you guessed it—another champagne house, where the prizes were handed out. We would get nothing due to no car, but we ended up with a large bottle of champagne, a golf umbrella, and a kiss each. On the way back to the hotel, Alain visited a friend of his who had his own vineyard. Jacques offered us grape juice and then champagne. It was so good that we both wished to buy some champgne. He gave us each a bottle, making it difficult to then buy. It had been specially made for the

Enilorac

millennium. I put Johanna's nose out of joint because of the "Auld Alliance" between the Scots and the French. Despite all that champagne, one was not drunk, and it tasted so much better than that which is exported.

The following morning, when the AA came to collect the car and us from the garage, the chief of police was there to see us off. We had to return by boat, and Johanna is not a good sailor, so she spent the entire journey flat on the deck. We like to get up to mischief together, and the older we are, the better it is. With all my friends, I have given medical advice informally, and sometimes I have been useful in this manner.

Throughout my life, I have a mixture of friends, some older and some younger than me. Since moving to the Borders, I have made friends with Clare, who is one of my neighbours. She is a strong-minded woman has become a close friend. We frequently ask each other for advice. Her man, David, is a qualified electrician but can turn his hand to anything except house painting; he is a very useful man to know. He has replaced Irish John (in Manchester; more later) for helping me. Although I am content to be on my own, sometimes not talking to anyone for some days, I gain much pleasure from the contact with my various friends. Even if I am not in constant communication with them, my friends are an important part of my life.

I have many acquaintances but probably four main friends: Jane, Ann in London, Johanna in Folkestone and now Winifred.

13

The Men in My Life

'Tis better to have loved and lost than never to have loved at all.
—Alfred, Lord Tennyson, *In Memoriam A.H.H.*

Throughout my life, I have had many female and male acquaintances and friends. Most were platonic, but not all. As Mummy once said about a fellow school teacher, a spinster after the war, "She'll not die wondering."

Male influences in my young life were my two grandfathers, Uncle Alan (he called me "Gasoline") and Uncle Sandy (whom I regarded as a father figure). I have already mentioned Cousin Bill, who also became a doctor (a paediatric cardiologist in Glasgow). We may not see each other during the year but are still connected. Ted (Teddy when he was younger) a cousin was a playmate in Arbroath, but contact was lost when our mothers fell out. I am happy that there has been a reconnection with him and his wife, Florrie, even though they live in the south of England.

None of his siblings survive, but he has three boys, now young men.

My good friend Lewis was never a boyfriend but was a great mate, although we lost touch as we grew up. He became a banker like his father. He lived in the south of England and was married with two boys. I was all over the place for various posts. On one occasion, we did meet in his mother's flat (a widow who was back teaching then), and his young children looked at us, amazed that we old fuddy-duddies had ever played together. He came back into my life when I retired back to Scotland.

When Edinburgh College had its five-hundred-year celebration in 2005–2006, the Scotsman newspaper had a supplement on the college's history. I was featured as being the first lady on council. The journalist wanted to know how old I was. I replied, "Women don't usually tell their age," to which he replied that all the others featured were dead. Collapse of me! Lewis read this article and wrote to the College, wondering if I was the Caroline Doig he had known, and contact was made. We met and eventually were joined by Ruth, another school friend from Forfar now residing in Edinburgh. Between us, we hatched the plan to have a class reunion around 2010. It was initially a lunch which later developed into a dinner. We involved those we could contact in and around our year at Forfar Academy, and Lewis got an article in the local Forfar paper. It worked very well and continues yearly, now run by others. We meet in Perthshire, which is convenient for Forfarians and those from the south. It is strange how little we have changed. We're older, yes, but with the same mannerisms. Some even came from abroad, and old friendships are revived, such as mine with Vivian. We have reconnected, to our delight. On hearing the short précis of the activities of our class since school, it is surprising that none of us have met at an airport because we are so well travelled. Although only a handful of us went to university, many got further qualifications. Some of us in and around Edinburgh met for lunch in the New Club throughout the year.

At university, I was "la dame formidable", or so I am told—tall, imposing, and determined. Very few of the lads were willing to take on the challenge. My friendship with Tom (one of the St Andrews crowd who joined us at the end of third year) has endured. We would talk well into the night about life and the future. I became a shoulder to cry on when he had girlfriend problems, and this has continued even now, though with different problems. He became an ENT surgeon in Reading in the same hospital as David, my magician friend from London—the shortest and tallest of my male friends. While in Dundee, Tom lived in a flat with two other friends: Tony, from our year and a fellow Lancastrian, and Mat a Dutch engineering student. My cabability to be a good listner continued and was and is used by many others.

A Yorkshire man from my year, Peter was thought to have the sexiest voice on the phone. I used to say I would go to Paris with him if he bought me an emerald ring, because we both wanted to go to Paris, and I have always liked emeralds. He never did, but we remain good friends. On my frequent car journeys up and down England, I would visit him and his wife, Greta. Again, my shoulder came into use when his wife died suddenly. The same goes for John (from London, now in Stirling) when his wife died. As a student,

Enilorac

he had once had Boxing Day lunch with Mother and me in Forfar because he had no money to go home to London.

One of the tall men in the year above from Jamaica, Derek, was a friend of Tom's and was my partner at a Westpark (female student residence) dance. It was so pleasant to have to look up to my partner. It was he who told me of my reputation later, when we demonstrated anatomy together. He washed my hair under the tap when I did not want it done—admittedly, I had given him cheek. We continued to keep in contact over the years, even after he emigrated to Canada. Sadly, he has died. He was another who said I should get married and have children—and so he was another who was disappointed that I never married. Another very tall man, Neil, was in the year ahead. For his comfort, he would send his own bed ahead when he moved jobs. He also partnered me at a Westpark dance.

While demonstrating in anatomy, I stayed in Westpark Hall as a sub-warden and did some anatomical research in cell mitosis, which was presented at an Anatomical Society meeting in Dundee. This was under the supervision of one of the lecturers, who believed that children should be born at sixteen years old. At the conference across the room, two people were able to see each other above the heads of others. This was David, later in Reading, whose hobby was magic, and me. He was and is a member of the Magic Circle. We met again when I went for an interview at GOS for a junior post, for which I was unsuccessful (the job going to a St Thomas's graduate who had never been interviewed for a post before). David came north, and for a few days I entertained him in St Andrews and at Pitlochry Theatre, and he entertained Mother with magic! On my return home one evening, she asked if he had kissed me, adding "Not that I want him to," I replied no, and she retorted, "What's wrong with him?" David reappeared when we met at the English College seniors meetings. At these meetings, a group of tall people sit together, where they can stretch their legs.

My first boyfriend was a chap in the year below me, but this did not last long. While working in Dundee, I met a former naval man from the north of Scotland. Duncan was good fun. He played rugby, and I watched him play. We went to an international at Murrayfield, and he was resplendent in his kilt. However, I left the area for another post, and so it ended. I was working as a junior doctor and even as a consultant, and so there was little time to socialise. When I managed to squeeze some time to do so, it was inevitably with other medics—a somewhat limited pool. It was not until my late twenties, working in Glasgow, that I lost my virginity to a married senior registrar. Unfortunately, this was to become a theme in my life. In medicine, women meet only doctors and very few non-medics and most of those she does meet are already married. The close proximity of working together in the hospital leads to such relationships, especially if the young male doctor married in haste.

In Glasgow, much to a senior nurse's disgust, Cousin Bill would take me out to dinner and once even to the hospital dance. I was resplendent in a blue and green ball gown. "Should never be seen except upon an Irish queen," one of the group was heard to say.

When I was a house physician in Dundee, I met another Bill, a junior consultant and bachelor. He invited me to the theatre, and we became an item. This continued when I returned to do my research post. Although he was considerably older than me, we were always able to talk about anything and everything. We even got to the stage of looking at engagement rings. But then I decided somehow it did not seem right. He suggested that I marry a rich, fat, greasy Greek. Why greasy and why Greek, I have no idea. This did not stop us from remaining friends, and we kept in touch so that on my return to Scotland after retirement, he would phone me on a Sunday evening, and we would discuss the world for an hour or more. He was always going to take me to lunch but never got round to it. He had never married but had numerous lady friends. He played the stock market quite successfully, and when he died, I found that he had left me a legacy and also made me one of his executors. One of the other executors, Mairi, was another of his ex-girlfriends, and we have become friends.

When I returned to Dundee in the late 1960s to do research, I had more free time and was staying in a bungalow with some other university friends. One of the girls (non-medical) who had been part of our university group asked if I could help her out. Her boyfriend's brother, Alan, had come home. They were due to go to a dance, but he did not have a partner. My first and only blind date was with this tall, good-looking merchant navy officer. We hit it off and continued to see each other throughout his leave. He did appear in Forfar when I was entertaining (or being entertained) by David (the member of the magic circle). Mother wondered what I was going to do with two men. It sorted itself out. Near the end of his leave, I was at a family party with both brothers, both of them playing footsie with me under the table. His brother, Robin, had split up with my friend. While his father was under the care of the ward where I worked, he asked me out. We had a fairly lengthy relationship which lasted until my move to Durham, but he was very possessive. One of his hobbies was fishing, but I never saw or knew him to catch anything.

When I worked briefly in Edinburgh, I reconnected with one of the dentists who had been in the same year. When we did anatomy as undergraduates, the dental students shared our teaching. He was working in the dental hospital and would take me out to dinner, although once he refused due to my wearing "a Chunky Chick", a coat I had made for myself! Once while walking along Chamber Street in Edinburgh, I was aware of a person coming in the opposite direction. It was Andy, one of the other dental students. Strangely enough, we continued to meet after that because we were both on the General Dental Council in London. I was there as a representative of the GMC. Yet another dentist, from Wolverhampton, did not renew our friendship after my faux pas. While listening to music on his car radio, I remarked that I liked the tune "Charade" but could not remember with whom I had seen the film. It had been him!

In Durham, it was possible to socialise with university people. I became friendly with a non-medical geography lecturer, who was small but good company. It was not until I started in GOS that we ended it. At a lunch in the Post Office Tower (then a restaurant), we fell out and I suggested he leave by the most rapid route—that is, the outside of the tower. Strangely, we had no further contact.

Two of us organised a Scandinavian-style party, with me doing the cooking and Jack providing the flat (much bigger), and the drinks. He also did the shopping but had

Enilorac

problems with my bad writing, and he misread "frozen prawns" for "prawn fingers". The party was a great success. Many of my colleagues were from all over the world: America, Czechoslovakia, Greece, and India, to name but a few. Lasting friendships were made.

Every year in the autumn at one of the livery halls, GOS held a dinner for consultants and junior staff. They were very elegant affairs in beautiful surroundings. In the Apothecaries Hall, one of the thoracic senior registrars, Ian, sat near me and introduced me to a fellow thoracic trainee. Ian had been my registrar in Dundee The two of them walked me home, and his friend was to feature later in my life.

Once I got the post in Manchester, I was busy in a different way: the buck stopped with me. I renewed my acquaintance with the urologist whom I had met during the English fellowship and his wife, Liz, while I was attached to one of the three academic surgical departments in Manchester.

I ended up working closely with a general surgeon, Rory, in the department. He had similar interests (e.g., the liver). He would frequently help when I had a patient with a problem more common in adults (e.g., pancreatic diseases). I became a shoulder to cry on again when his first marriage (and also the second one) broke down. We would meet at meetings, have the occasional meal, or drink together. One time, he took me to the Grand National at Aintree.

While working in Manchester, I was phoned by Humphrey (from my year and ex-golf partner), asking to come to Brighton, where he was surprising his wife, Aileen, with a party. When he asked John (one of our university year from London) to give a speech, he demurred, and so I ended up doing it. Humph always talked too much, and I had to say, "Shut up!" He did—to the surprise of most of the people there. They said, "You must know him very well!"

Because paediatric surgery is a small sub-speciality, people know each other well, and I would be able to go anywhere in the world knowing the local paediatric surgeon on first-name terms. I naturally gravitated towards the Scandinavians, who were tall and blonde like me. I had previously met an Abereen graduate, Toby, from Trondheim at a meeting in England. He returned to Trondheim with his wife, an Aberdonian, and became professor of paediatric surgery. He and his wife are still good friends with me.

Apart from attending paediatric surgical meetings here and abroad, I also attended general surgical meetings and made many friends. This proved to be useful in my medical political life. At such a meeting in Sheffield, I met Johnny, who smoked a pipe (or as I said, matches). We immediately hit it off and arranged to meet again. He was of course married, but he was about to leave his wife when he became ill. While I was away at meetings in Europe, he died. I was devastated and rushed headlong into a messy relationship with an alcoholic university fellow. It did not last.

By now, I was involved with the Edinburgh College, and I renewed my friendship with various surgeons. I had first met one of them with Mother at a meeting in Aberdeen. We continued to meet at college functions and worked on council together. He was a widower, and we developed a deep friendship which has lasted even after I was no longer closely involved in the college.

Although I never married, I had many male acquaintances and friends many of whom are still in contact.

As for children, apart from all those I treated and looked after, I am godmother to four. In my life, I have only loved three men: one died, one remarried unsuccessfully, and one remarried successfully. I am happy with my life.

Although I am frequently alone, I am never lonely.

Toby (my Norwegian friend) and I

Andrew and Mother in Hungary

In Lebanon at Christmas time with Samir and Madeleine

Mother in the Jockey Club room at
Shatin racecourse, Hong Kong

Scuba diving on the Great Barrier Reef

Giving a College lecture overseas

With a tiger in New Delhi wearing my new Indian clothes

Some of the Edinburgh Council members at
the Taj Mahal with bare feet in the rain

Daddy's tombstone in Stellawood cemetry
in Durban, South Africa

Vivian and I at school reunion more than 70 years later

Winifred and I not driving a Vespa

Johanna's car -I am not driving

Derek and I at Westpark Student Dance

Rory and I at a conference dinner

Mother with a dog- and pure white hair in Guernsey

Edinburgh Doll house Club at show in Edinburgh

14

Mother

For you are the wind beneath my wings Jeff Silbar & Larry Henley *Bette Midler song*

Mother had an unhappy childhood, although she adored her father, and that was followed by a short but very happy married life. Then Mother had to get on with the hard graft of bringing up a young child on her own during the war and having to earn a living at the same time. I think if it had not been for me to look after, she would have joined the Forces and died during the war. She had nothing to live for, and so I became her raison d'être.

She was always my support and help, loving me unconditionally. She was subjected to being a model for surface anatomy. When possible, she would give me what I wanted, even when money was short. I learnt not to ask for anything and everything, and to relish what I did get. However, I was not spoilt, at least not by her. I had a happy childhood because she was determined that I would not suffer as she had. Cuddles were common. She had a lot to put up with from a determined and occasion wayward daughter. Once during junior school, I brought my friends to see her. At the time, she had an enormous nose because she had been bitten by a horsefly!

We did everything together, including shopping after school and having high tea at a variety of different restaurants. Every morning, she was up early to clean the house and prepare for the day. People remarked that we were more like sisters than mother and daughter. Certainly we were good friends with a relationship the envy of my friends. I could and did tell her everything. We did have massive rows; two determined women with their own minds were always going to meet head-on. But it always sorted itself out, and I do not remember either of us giving way. When working in Durham, after a phone call to Mummy that ended in a tiff, my colleague said she had never had a row with her mother. I thought this indicated a subservient relationship—not good. You are only really angry with someone you love.

She helped with my dressmaking and knitting. She was an excellent embroiderer and also did crochet. She tried to teach me this, but had to give up because I was hopeless. Teaching me bridge was another ambition doomed to failure, despite it being a "social asset"! We did play other card games, cribbage and bezique, as well as Scrabble.

During summer holidays, we once went to a beauty demonstration in one of the local church halls. When the lady doing the demonstration on one of the local women remarked about how moist our skins were, we had to leave early. "A lot of Wets" was Mother's remark, at which we laughed too much. I have inherited her lovely smooth skin, helping me to look younger than I am.

Holidays were usually in Scotland, but our first trip abroad was to Copenhagen when I was working in Glasgow. She loved the city and the smell of cigars. When I was in Durham, we took a Fred Olsen line ship to Oslo, using the boat as a hotel. She was still an attractive woman and had trouble with a fellow passenger who followed her around until she loudly told him to go back to his wife.

A car trip round the whole of Ireland was hilarious. In the south, the hotel we had booked was unsatisfactory, and so we found one by Bantry bay. On the way into it, a notice stated, "Beware twins and turkeys." The owner of the hotel had been one of the first Europeans into Tibet. I could not find reception but was directed to a box room, where stood a barefooted man with a monocle. On asking about accommodation, he said, "Ah, bless you, my dear, for your lovely Scotch voice," and we were in, even if the leprechauns sometimes forgot to put on the hot water. The kitchen was run by his wife, an excellent cook. The head waiter never wrote any orders down, but it was always right. We were served superbly by what we called Valkyries, who wore blouses that once were white, held together by safety pins. We could sit outside by the water's edge while Mother was hidden by a huge Labrador on her lap. A gentleman looking like something out of Dickens sailed across the bay to what he called his *local*. The owner did not like Americans, but on one occasion he had one who complained about the Mateus Rose being flat. In a temper, the colonel (the owner) grabbed the bottle and stormed out to the dining room, saying, "I don't care what she wants—we don't have it." No one criticised his wine cellar. The rest of us in the bar (our usual haunt after dinner) knew we had to do something to change the mood. A tall, thin man (something in the Foreign Office) asked for an Irish coffee and then stated it was flat! After a pause, the colonel laughed, and all was right with the world.

The bar had a series of rude French cartoons bought in France and also a rare French brandy which Mother liked. She spent the rest of her life trying to find it but was never successful. When we left, Mummy was kissed by him—a rare compliment.

Following an operation, Mother recuperated in Durham, staying in a hotel. It meant that when I was off duty, we could tour around the north-east, which has marvellous scenery and loads of places to visit. She was by the river Wear and started to draw and paint again. I have said earlier that she wished to go to art college, but in the mid-twenties this was not deemed suitable for a young girl, and in any case, her mother did not wish this. She did very well at senior school, and I still have two paintings done by her at school, which hang on my wall at home. After being unsuccessful (although she had tried to see the head of the college), she did not draw anymore, except when teaching eight- and nine-year-olds. Durham was the first time she got back into sketching. Later, when her eyesight deteriorated (she developed macular degeneration), she stopped despite my comments that it would be interesting to see what she saw!

While I worked in London, she would winter with me, looking after me and occasionally exploring London on her own. She was retired and so could spend the whole season with me before returning home in the spring. The greengrocers (cockney lads) took a liking to her, and one Christmas they gave her a pot with bulbs-for nothing.

Initially she was loath to travel beyond the local shops, which were like a village around the hospital. Soon she started to go farther afield, even managing to get lost on her way back from Tottenham Court Road. She had no sense of direction. She sometimes looked after Ann's firstborn but had problems. It had been many years since she had changed a nappy, and she could not work out how to get at the baby through the Babygro.

We would visit Covent Garden and various theatres. Like me, she was very fond of ballet, and once we managed to see Rudolf Nuryev and Margot Fonteyn. We were adopted by Parsley, a cat belonging to the people next door. When he was told off, he would retreat to our flat, meowing at the balcony door. Despite being more of a dog person (having been brought up with gun dogs), she fell for him until she upset him by inadvertently sitting on him. It took him a long time to come back after that. At the end of winter, we would go north, zigzagging up England. Occasionally I could manage some time off, and we visited the Cotswolds and some of the West Country. We even managed a holiday to Guernsey, where she had a great time with a black dog. She always wanted to have a dog of her own. We even decided on a dachshund with the name Wagner, but with a flat on the second floor, no garden, and us both being out most of the day, this was not possible. By the time it might have happened, she was too unwell and I was too busy.

She came with me to many BAPS meetings, attending the ladies programme so often she knew more of the city than I did. She came to Berne and also Vienna. When we went to Vienna, my colleague Joe was also attending but was flying out of Heathrow with a different airline. It was a

Enilorac

time when one had to indicate one's luggage on the tarmac before it could be placed on the plane. On our arrival from the Manchester flight, our luggage was not there. We were told to get on the flight anyway. I was wearing a turquoise jumpsuit that Mother loathed, and she kept looking at me and muttering. On arrival at Vienna, strangely our cases were there, having been put on the wrong plane (with Joe's luggage) and arriving before us. I could change my clothes! This happened again recently when Winifred and I returned from Hungary.

On the spur of the moment, we decided to go to Gibraltar. She did not have her passport with her, asking, "Do I need one?" We had sent a telegram to her neighbours (they had no phone) to get them to ring us from our flat in Forfar so that she could tell them about the passport and they could send it to her. Apart from her sitting on her spectacles and the involvement with the navy, we went to Tangiers as a separate trip organised in Gibraltar. She adored the fresh oranges (peeled by a Rif) and hated the camels—they spit!

When I became a consultant in Manchester, she came to live with me. I had said that I wanted her furniture for my house, and she said that meant her too. Until ill health and age prevented her, she acted as my housekeeper and cook. Once when I had to cancel an outing, yet again, because of a neonatal emergency, she remarked that if she had been married to me, she would have left me!

I persuaded her (against her own inclination) to help me organise various parties and dinners. Because of her childhood, she lacked confidence, but she would thoroughly enjoy herself into being the life and soul of the party. When he was alive, Daddy had started to develop a jewellery collection for her. I continued this once I was earning enough. Of course, there was an ulterior motive because I would inherit all her jewellery when she died. In Edinburgh, we bought a pair of earrings together; she owned one, and I owned the other.

She came with me to paediatric surgical conferences in Hungary (as explained earlier), Chios, and Jersey (where she had spent her honeymoon). She also attended general surgical meetings (e.g., in Dundee when we were living in Manchester). On the ladies programme there, she went to a whisky distillery. She did not like whisky, and so I was surprised when she returned with a couple of bottles of Glenturret (no longer available), which was excellent. The distillery had exported to the States in the Twenties and so were hit badly with prohibition, but they were on the up and up.

After some time in a townhouse, it became obvious that the stairs were a problem for her, and so we moved to a semi-detached nearby with a garden. When we moved, we were put in touch with a Irish handyman, John. He could turn his hand to anything and even helped when I locked us both out. Neither was that the first time I had problems. I had been gardening and wished to show Mummy my efforts. When I pushed the wheelchair into the garden, I inadvertently locked us in the garden. I had to climb over the back fence into wasteland to reach our neighbours, who had a ladder. Then I climbed back into the garden with the ladder and climbed up to the balcony and bedroom window—and I do not have a head for heights. All this happened on a hot summer's day, with me wearing very short bright pink shorts.

Enilorac

The garden at the new house was not developed, and between us we consulted gardening books and went to garden centres so that I could make it a haven for birds and Mummy. We went regularly to Martin Mere, a Wildfowl and Wetland reserve. Even when she was in a wheelchair, she enjoyed the visits and her beloved nenes (Hawaiian geese). I developed a lasting interest in birds.

One evening she had a profuse nose bleed. Despite my efforts, it continued, and so I took her to casualty in my own hospital, a children's hospital. Here the consultant ENT surgeon managed to stop the bleed in the anteroom to theatre. I pointed out that she was far too old for that hospital, at eighty-five years. Her reply was, "No, I'm not. I'm 8 point 5, so that's okay!" There was laughter all round.

She was totally deaf in one ear following a mastoid operation after the war, and so I would place her in company with me on her deaf side. With age, her good ear started to deteriorate, and she became deaf in both ears. We invested in a portable microphone, which was placed in the centre of the table. When anyone wanted to speak to her (which was often), they would grab the microphone. It was also useful in the car by shutting out the extraneous noises. This new deafness was probably as a result of transient ischaemic attacks (TIAs), or mini strokes. Without her hearing aids, she was totally deaf. She used this to her advantage when we were arguing by smiling sweetly at me and turning her hearing aids off—adding to my frustration!

She was inordinately proud of my achievements but always had a dry wit to keep me grounded. When the then president of the Edinburgh college at a college dinner acknowledged my appointment as first lady, she said, "On your own heads be it." She loved going to college functions, even when she was in a wheelchair. A chairlift had been installed for one of the regents of the college, but Mother hanselled it(used it first). She would be kept amused by the then minister of St Giles Church telling her his wicked stories. I am hoping he will still be around to bury me.

We travelled with the college all over the world: Kuala Lumpur, Singapore (which she loved, especially the orchids), and Hong Kong (even when she was in a wheelchair, although she found it claustrophobic). On one occasion, she taught an American surgeon how to use chopsticks. In Singapore we discovered a Ming factory, where they made genuine reproductions! She was very fond of blue and white china, and so she loved this.

As she entered her eighties, she became less able. The first indication was an episode of breathlessness as she was climbing a steep slope in Edinburgh. She had major heart problems which got worse with age, eventually leading to her final admission to hospital.

In the March before she died, I was due to examine in Hong Kong but could not leave Mother because of her ill health. She was determined to go, however, even although she was unwell on the morning of our departure. I had arranged for business travel and our room to be available on arrival. She slept the entire journey; I got no sleep. On arrival, she had not had a meal on the plane and was hungry, and so we had brunch. I hoped we could then go to bed, but she said, "We are in Hong Kong. Aren't we going shopping?" I wearily pushed her around the mall, and she eventually wished to go to bed. The hotel staff were very good at looking after her while I was working, so she would be well rested and ready for the evening's entertainment. At one such function, she took the fancy of a small, grey-haired Chinese surgeon who would pat her head, much to her chagrin. On my return to Hong Kong alone after her death, he greeted me but was looking behind me for her wheelchair!

Once she was no longer able to look after me, it was time for me to look after her. If I was away for a short time, Irene would stay overnight. They both liked this arrangement, and Irene heard stories about various objects. On one occasion, the husband of my best friend phoned to talk with me. Somewhat put out when Irene answered the phone, he asked who she was. "Miss Doig's secretary. Would you like to speak with Mrs Doig?" Mother did not want to speak to "that creep". Unfortunately, although Irene had covered the phone, he still heard. When he did speak with me, he remarked that my mother did not like him!

Mother liked to entertain the numerous overseas doctors who came to train with me. She was especially pleased when an Indian doctor complimented her on her cooked rice. Edward (from Malawi) and Samir (from Lebanon) were firm favourites. She did enjoy travelling and at long last was happy meeting people.

She went downhill fairly rapidly and was admitted to Manchester Royal Infirmary in May 1997. It was obvious that she was seriously ill and could not come to Irene's wedding. I managed the service but not the reception. I arranged for her to meet a minister, the husband of one of my theatre sisters (Church of England, with there being no Church of Scotland in Manchester), a delightful man we both had met before. I warned him that she did not like ministers; her experiences in Forfar had coloured her opinions. He and his wife appeared, and we talked for a while before Mother said, "If I want a minister, I would not mind John." "Do you need one?" I replied. "Not just now." This was two days before she died. His wife and I left the room, leaving them together. I do not know what transpired, but after they left, she remarked that she had wanted to talk to a minister. Why had she not said?

She died in the hospital with me beside her on St Columba's Day 1997. John helped with the funeral when she was cremated. Another help was from Liz, the wife of an urologist friend. Mother had fallen out with her remaining sister over a thank-you letter. I had only just got her to send Christmas cards, and so I knew Mother would not want her at the funeral. Liz took a letter I wrote and posted it; I do not know when.

I did manage to meet up with Auntie Elma before she died, and I found that her youngest child, a solicitor, was also interested in doll's houses like me—strange. I made sure that her coffin was covered in flowers; she adored wildlife, and her only school medal was for botany.

Samir, our Lebanese friend, wanted to come to the funeral, but I would not allow him. It consisted of my Doig cousins, Irene, my trainees of the time, and handyman John. Six months later, Auntie Mary (my Doig cousins' mother) died. Now I was alone, having lost my best friend and mother. It took some time to remember to shop for one and not two. Although I had thought about returning to Scotland, I decided to wait until 2000 before retiring. Too much change in life's course at one time would have been traumatic.

15

Third Life

They are not long, the days of wine and roses.
—Ernest Dowson, *They Are Not Long*

As changes occurred in the NHS that were not to my liking, I decided to retire early. Mother dying aged eighty-seven in 1997 meant that I delayed the decision because I needed to keep myself occupied. I had to fight for beds when I'd started, and I did not expect to be doing the same twenty-five years later. My birthday in April 2000 had a nice ring to it, so that was when I retired. Surgeons find it difficult to stop work, as evidenced by my colleague Joe Cohen. By finishing work and laying aside my scalpel in 2000, but continuing my medical political life, it allowed me to slow down, finishing my college council work in 2001 and finishing with the GMC two years later.

My last week was organised to be not too strenuous, with only minor cases for surgery. That was until one of my colleagues asked me to stand in for him while he attended a legal case. He was on call but would be back by evening.

He could pick up any problems on his return, and so this should not be too taxing, especially because I was detailed to go for dinner with friends. Fate had other ideas. Around lunchtime, I was requested to see a teenager on the medical ward. He was known to suffer from Crohn's disease (IBD) and had been ill for some days. He had only just presented at the hospital. He was very seriously ill, requiring urgent resuscitation before surgery could be performed. By late afternoon, although he was slightly better, it was obvious that he needed urgent surgery—I could not wait for my colleague's return. While the anaesthetist (who was very short) was putting him to sleep, he arrested. Fortunately, because of the presence of the anaesthetist and the senior paediatrician, he was quickly resuscitated—but then he arrested again. The anaesthetist asked if I could operate while he was still on the trolley because they were wary of moving him on to the operating table. The operating table can be adjusted in height, but not the trolley. It was okay for him but not for my six feet height. When I opened him up, the bowel had burst with gross inflammation. Surgery would have to be quick and damage-limiting—nothing fancy, only removal of the dead bowel and a stoma. I successfully carried it out, and he was transferred to the high care unit. My colleague returned, and I passed the patient over to his long-term care. I was delighted to hear later that after further reconstructing surgery, the patient did well and went home with no ill effects some weeks later.

While waiting for my colleague to return, I had arranged to meet on the ward with the senior lecturer in general surgery (who I had operated with on numerous occasions) who had been requested to see a child with pancreatitis.

When I finished operating, I realised that he had not appeared, but he was a notoriously poor time keeper. The next day, he phoned and asked if I usually operated around the level of my knees! He had appeared at the operating theatre door, but no one saw him—not the anaesthetist, nurse, or runner. Realising that matters were tense, he left. That was the last operation I ever carried out.

Later that week, the ward organised a party for me. With Irene's help, they had managed to contact many of the patients who had been my most testing and major cases over the years. It was a marvellous experience, and they had produced a book with pictures. Many were working in a variety of different occupations, even nursing. A few were married, and one appeared with his new baby. This was especially pleasing because he had been very ill with ulcerative colitis, requiring extensive surgery in the pelvis with the added risk of damage to important nerves. Obviously, I had left them intact.

On the first Monday of my new life, I organised a course of golf lessons. Although I had played as a schoolgirl, there was never enough time while I was in training. This did not improve once I was a consultant, managing perhaps one game a year. I had played with a fellow Scot, Ian, but we met on the tee and the green because he went wildly from side to side, and I dribbled up the fairway. I required a lot of help to correct the mistakes I had developed over the years.

It was strange not having to get up early, and my time was not organised minute by minute. Quite soon I was being told by friends that I looked ten years younger due to the lack of stress. I could have lunch (often with Liz) instead of rushing between hospitals. I could now do what I wanted when I wanted, and I indulged in my hobbies: golf, swimming, cooking, gardening, and reading. I could learn to draw and paint—something I had always wanted to learn. Do I have the talent that Mother had? No, but I enjoy it.

Although I was an honorary red rose (after twenty-five years in Manchester), I realised that there was very little reason for staying in Manchester because I had no great affinity for most of my then colleagues. Friends would come and see me wherever I ended up. I could not see me being an old lady in Manchester, and I wanted to return to Scotland. As far as I knew, there was no one left in my hometown, Forfar, whom I knew. However, I did have connections in Edinburgh through the college, the Medical Women's Federation, and school friends. Unfortunately, at that time in the late nineties, Edinburgh was very expensive. I became despondent until it was pointed out to me that, because I would no longer be working, I did not require to be in the city but could widen my search to the surrounding area. When I came to Edinburgh for college meetings, I would stay longer and look at houses. I told friends in Manchester that I would be there for a further two years, but two months after I retired, I found and bought a lovely cottage in a small village in the Borders, in Heriot. My own house in Manchester was not even on the market, so I did not move until September. I could measure and decide matters on my visits to Edinburgh. With help from friends in Manchester (Carys, a neurosurgeon, and Ian, my golf partner), we moved certain things (such as doll's houses) before the actual move.

The cottage is in the grounds of a large Victorian house in what had been outbuildings. There is a sense of community, with the ladies running a book club. In the spring, there is a bank of snowdrops, and I have regular visits of pheasants to my garden. Numerous other birds come to my bird table: all sorts of tits, chaffinches, blackbirds, a robin, a woodpecker, and even a nuthatch. I have become an ardent bird watcher with the RSPB and the Scottish Ornithological group, going on educational outings with them.

Johanna had been at a college dinner and was persuaded to come house hunting afterwards, when we saw my cottage and both liked it. She spent the first New Year celebration with me in the snow. The snow gates were closed, making it impossible to go to a Hogmanay party in the city. We were turned back by a policeman. "It's a very long time since I've been told to go home by a policeman," she said. I had been told that snow was rarely a problem, yet in that first year, I was both snowed in and snowed out. On returning from London, my neighbour, Clare, told me that there was a six-foot snow drift opposite the village hall, and so I required urgent accommodation in the already full George Hotel. The snow adds to the feeling of isolation but brings out the feeling of community as we help each other.

At this time, I was still required to attend council meetings in Edinburgh and go to Manchester and London for GMC matters. This allowed me to unwind slowly because without clinical work, I was still involved in committee work. I thought I would miss the children and the operating, but I did not. It was obviously the right time to retire. The only one I missed was my secretary, Irene.

Shortly after Mother died, John, our odd-job man, was sorting out things in the house. I asked him to check the roof and tell me what was in the attic. I do not have a head for heights, and access was via a Ramsay ladder. Amongst other things he mentioned was the doll's house that Daddy had made for me. We took it down, and I started to sort it, eventually finding a shop whose owner was most helpful and buying a couple of books. Daddy's house was a bungalow in the 1930s style, and so I set out to repair it. Soon afterwards, I told Johanna I was sorting the bathroom and was about to repair the roof. After a pause, she said, "Don't fall off the roof." She was relieved when I clarified it was a doll's house roof. So started my addiction. I was given a Georgian house by the hospital when I retired. I became a member of the South Manchester Doll House Club and now am a member of the club in Edinburgh, which displays at an annual show. I now have fourteen houses and over twenty-one room boxes (some of them reflecting my previous life), housed in a special room. Initially I did not wish to have people in them, but now I enjoy making clothes for the less--than-six-inch people. Winter nights are filled with that or sewing carpets for the various houses. It is pleasant to be doing things with my hands and meeting non-medics.

As a child, I would read voraciously, sometimes being unaware of my surroundings. In Heriot, we have a ladies' book club, and I continue to read avidly on a variety of subjects. I could go to see plays at the theatre and enjoy ballets, operas (my favourite being *Tosca*) knowing that I would not be called away. The same goes for concerts, which I attend frequently in Usher Hall in Edinburgh in the winter months. Now I had time to play golf regularly (with Winifred, as indicated earlier). We also joined an art group, Art Out and About, which meets on a Tuesday afternoon. Although I have no talent, I have improved and do enjoy it.

Enilorac

Another activity was a cooking class run by the University of the Third Age. We were taught by an Australian girl of Italian origin who married to a Scot and has travelled all over the world. Although the class has sadly stopped, I still use Susie's recipes.

Although I do not travel to London as often as I did, I go to the seniors meeting of the English College, which usually has an interesting visit before the actual meeting eg to Horse Quards parade, Thomas Coram's house or Charterhouse. I can stay with Ann and we explore. Once she managed to get tickets to the Chelsea Flower show, which was crowded—but oh, the flowers! I try to organise to see Johanna too on these occasions. Although initially I was loath to get involved in gardening, I soon became interested and could not pass a garden centre without buying something. This meant a garden was important when I was looking at houses in Edinburgh.

The one in Heriot where I live now is of a reasonable size, but I am now unable to tend the garden myself due to my back problems. I have had several people do most of the work, but it is difficult to get anyone to do it for any length of time. Since my PE (see later), I have also needed help with the housework, but I have been more fortunate with this. A small Italian lady, Maria, now looks after me, organises my house, and makes me less sordid (as Mother once said of my living conditions so many years ago).

I enjoy travel, and with Winifred I can indulge myself, travelling mostly by boat on rivers. Although she does not like to swim, when possible I will swim. Swimming in the beautiful, warm, blue Mediterranean seas is so pleasant, as opposed to the cold, grey Moray Firth.

In my late twenties, I was diagnosed as having bilateral duplex kidneys, but they have never given me any problems. Unfortunately, the scoliosis which was diagnosed at the same time has caused major problems. Because I stood to operate most of the time, my weight was distributed incorrectly. This only started to cause problems after my retirement. Investigations of my back problems have revealed osteoarthritis, but only of that part of my spine involved in the bend, which causes me almost continuos pain. I have no arthritis anywhere else; my hands, knees and hips are clear. Because of having broken both wrists, I had a bone scan done which showed osteopenia—that is, not quite osteoporosis but going that way. The back pain has got worse with a compression fracture of one of the vertebrea of my lower spine. As a result of this and my scoliosis getting worse, I am now only five feet nine inches tall instead of six feet.

I was relatively healthy most of my life (apart from appendicitis as a teenager), and it was not until March 2011 that I experienced more problems. While walking along Princes Street, I had pain in my right calf. It is very difficult to diagnose oneself. Was it deep venous thrombosis or a sprain? I felt well, and it seemed to get better, so I decided that it was a sprain. However, three days later, I coughed up a minute speck of blood. I remembered my teachings on this, and because I had no symptoms of breathlessness or pain, I thought that I probably had had a mini pulmonary infarct. I phoned the GP and got a neighbour to drive me to the hospital, where I walked up the stairs to the ward.

After investigations, I saw the consultant. I told him that I nearly did not phone the doctor. His reply was, "If you hadn't, I would not be speaking to you now." I had extensive bilateral

Enilorac

pulmonary emboli (PE), with pressure on the heart. This diagnosis usually means death. After I saw the report, I had to agree. I felt a fraud in the high dependency unit for the five days I was in hospital. At follow-up, my respiratory tests were better than they should be for my age, but then, I had never smoked and so probably had good residual lung function. I had always had an irregular heartbeat but was now found to have atrial fibrillation, necessitating me being on Warfarin for the rest of my life. This does not cause me any problems.

As I got older, I realised I had become less active, doing more sedentary things like embroidering cushions, tapestries, and miniature doll house carpets. I now attend a special gym class for people with problems, and this has helped. I call us the Golden Oldies. When possible, I go to the lunchtime meetings of the seniors club in the Edinburgh College of Surgeons. We occasionally meet with the same group from the College of Physicians.

Staying in the Borders so near Edinburgh (eighteen miles) means that I have a constant stream of visitors, old friends, friends from Manchester, and former trainees. Having a lovely garden and liking cooking meant I could entertain happily. I have been fortunate that throughout my life, I have made lasting friendships with people of both sexes, and although we may not make contact frequently, the connection is always there.

At Christmastime, Rachel and Bill, my Doig cousins, come to me, or I go to them. Occasionally Janet, their younger sister, gets involved; she lives with her husband, John, outside London. All three of their children are married and have children, and so it is a happy time. On one such occasion, we all went to the Albert Hall for a carol service. Unfortunately,

Rachel was sick. That was not the end of the drama because Bill started to have rigors in the night—a sign of infection. Eventually, John and I got him to a nearby hospital, which looked after him very well. As luck would have it, he was under the care of a friend of mine, a general surgeon who (with his wife) had attended English College meetings with me. Bill got better and eventually came home to Glasgow.

I have inherited Mother's white hair, and I hope that like her, I keep all my marbles. To help with this, I keep reading and doing crosswords and other brain teasers. In the past, I have attended classes at the university in Latin, picking up where I was when I was not allowed to take it further at school. I also attended Gaelic classes for three years. Despite our excellent teacher, I have no talent for languages and was not very good. Although I have a computer, I consider myself computer illiterate, often needing help from Winifred or neighbours.

Apart from the school reunions, a group of us meet in the New Club; I became a member after giving up the Lansdowne Club in London. There is also the university reunions, the last being in Cambridge. I drove there but organised it so that I had frequent stops—with Ram and Radica in Leeds, staying with Jane in Rushden—before the meeting. Afterwards, I went to an English college meeting in Wales in Llandudno before turning north to stay with Irene in Manchester on my way home. I do like driving, but that journey horrified Johanna when I told her about it.

A couple of years ago, during the disruption caused by the building of the Waverley railway line, a car drove into the side of my car one Sunday morning. The car was deemed a write-off, but apart from bruises I was okay because my airbag had worked. This necessitated a new car. It was only my second road accident in over fifty years.

As I have got older, I have become less impatient, but it still does rear its ugly head. Perhaps that was what was wrong at the GMC. I do not mind growing old—it is a privilege—but I wish I did not have to suffer the other things that come with old age, such as backache.

It is becoming obvious that as I get older and more decrepit, my lovely cottage in the country is less convenient. I would be very isolated if I could no longer drive, and so a move into Edinburgh will become necessary. I now have a second property, a penthouse flat with a terrace in the city. Apparently lots of my friends were worried about my potential isolation in the Borders. This will be much easier to manage when I move to Edinburgh, and I can still enjoy the theatre, concerts, and my friends. This move was all made possible by the legacy left to me by my ex-boyfriend William.

Who knows what the future will bring? I have inherited Mother's white hair, osteoporosis, and hopefully lack of dementia, and I hope to live as long as she did, to eighty-seven years or even longer. She was able the night before she died to tell me off for preventing her from doing what she wished.

I hope "Sans teeth, sans eyes, sans everything" will be much later. In the meantime, I am happy with life and look forward. Many years ago in Cullen, a fortune teller told me I would have many children. That was wrong, unless you count all my patients. She also said that I would live to be ninety-seven, so …..

Timeline

1909, November: Daddy's birth
1910, March: Mummy's birth
1937, July: Wedding of May and George
1938, April: My birth
1942, November: Daddy's death
1944: Betty's death
1943: School
1947: Mother's ear operation
1950: Senior school
1956. October: University
1962: Graduation
1962–63: Junior house jobs
1963–64: Anatomy demonstrator
1964, May: Primary fellowship
1964–65: Darlington SHO
1965-66 Glasgow SHO posts
1966–68: Research post
1967, January: FRCS Edinburgh
1968–70: Registrar, Durham
1970 FRCS England
1970 ChM
1970–75: Senior registrar, London

1975, August: Consultant in Manchester
1980: Examiner in primary fellowship
1982: Examiner Fellowship, Edinburgh College
1984–89: On Edinburgh council
1985–86: President, MWF
1989–94: Elected to GMC
1989–94: Re-elected to Edinburgh council
1994–99: Re-elected to GMC
1996–2001: Re-elected to Edinburgh council
1997, June: Mother's death
2000. April: Retirement
2011, March: Pulmonary Emboli

Lightning Source UK Ltd.
Milton Keynes UK
UKHW042103041218
333469UK00001B/9/P